LAWNS
NATURAL
and
ORGANIC

Don Williamson

LONE
PINE

Lone Pine Publishing International

The Distributor:
Lone Pine Publishing
1808 B Street NW, Suite 140
Auburn, WA, USA 98001

Website: www.lonepinepublishing.com

Library and Archives Canada Cataloguing in Publication

Williamson, Don, 1962-
    Lawns natural and organic / Don Williamson.

Includes index.

ISBN-13: 978-976-8200-14-3
ISBN-10: 976-8200-14-6

1. Lawns--United States.   2. Turf management--United States.
3. Organic gardening--United States.   I. Title.

SB433.15.W54 2005   635.9'64784'0973   C2005-906708-X

Scanning & Digital Film: Elite Lithographers Co.

Photography: **Accuproducts International** 82b; **Alison Beck** 43a, 48; **Alan Bibby** 160 insert; **Joan de Grey** 160 full frame; **Tamara Eder** 17, 39a&b, 65, 76, 83b, 90–91, 102, 111, 132, 139, 143a,b&c, 145a&b; **Derek Fell** 1, 11, 12, 14, 24, 29a, 31, 33, 36, 45, 58, 60, 61, 68a, 69, 73, 105, 148; **Erika Flatt** 20, 89; **Gardena Canada** 63b, 67a,b&c, 68b, 77a&b, 80a,b&c, 83a; **Anne Gordon** 13, 18, 84; **James A. Gordon** 44, 59; **Duncan Kelbaugh** 74; **Tim Matheson** 19, 37b, 53a, 95, 101, 113, 131, 138b, 142a&b, 144a&b; **Allison Penko** 114, 142c; **Laura Peters** 21a, 57b, 72, 96b, 97, 98a&b, 99a, 138a, 146b,c&d, 147a,b,c,d&e, 150; **Photos.com** 7, 8a, 15, 16, 103, 106, 107, 109, 140; **Robert Ritchie** 57a, 122; **Soil Foodweb Inc.** 87, 93a,b&c; **TPI** 23, 27, 28, 29b, 32, 34, 35, 70, 75a&b, 151; **Don Williamson** 8b, 9, 10, 21b, 22, 26, 37a,c&d, 38, 40a,b&c, 41a,b,c&d, 42a,b&c, 43b&c, 46, 49a&b, 50, 51a,b&c, 52, 53b, 54, 55a&b, 56a,b,c&d, 62, 63a&c, 71, 78, 79, 81, 82a, 92, 96a, 99b, 100, 104, 120, 124, 126, 127, 128, 129, 146a.

Front Cover Photo: Tamara Eder

PC: 13

Table of Contents

Selected Charts, Illustrations and Other Information

Acknowledgments

I STAND ON THE SHOULDERS OF GIANTS. The information in this book is the result of the efforts of many dedicated people, and I am honored to present it here.

My appreciation and thanks go to the following people for their invaluable aid in making sure the information in this book is as accurate as possible: Jack Wetmore, owner and founder of Wetmore's Landscaping Sod & Nursery of Island View, New Brunswick; Dr. Elaine Ingham, Matthew Slaughter and the folks at Soil Foodweb, Inc. in Corvallis, Oregon; Aimee Code, Megan Kemple, Kay Rumsey and the folks at Northwest Coalition for Alternatives to Pesticides (NCAP) in Eugene, Oregon; James Novak of Turfgrass Producers International in East Dundee, Illinois; and Andrew Dumbrille and the Sierra Club of Canada.

Special thanks for photographs and illustrations go to: James Novak, T. Kirk Hunter and the wonderful folks at Turfgrass Producers International; Jay Sterling, Liviana Macoretta and Gardena Canada, Ltd. for the pictures of their lawn and garden maintenance equipment (I personally use Gardena watering equipment); John Kosmalski and Accuproducts International (www.accuproducts.com) for the manual aerator; Anne and James Gordon, Duncan Kelbaugh and Derek Fell for the nice lawns; and Lone Pine photographers Tim Matheson, Tamara Eder, Erika Flatt, Robert Ritchie and Allison Penko. Thanks also to Lone Pine authors Laura Peters and Alison Beck.

I also thank the following wonderful folks who volunteered their time, effort and/or lawns to this book: Christian Houle, Olivier Le Tynevez-Dobel (and crew) and Terra Landscaping of Edmonton, AB; Rick and Tanya Van Papeveld; Kimberlee and Grant Bawolin; K&M Bobcat Services in Legal, AB; Frank Cadieux and crew of AM-PM Group Construction & Landscaping Division of Edmonton, AB; Stuart Franklin of Nature's Lawn and Garden, Inc. in Buffalo, NY; Julie Tobler and the folks at Jacklin Seed in Post Falls, ID; Stan Haraskiewicz and Heritage Earthworks Contracting, Ltd. in St. Albert, AB; Bill Haydey; Doug Kruger; Diana and Jay Trembley; Rob Witherspoon at the Guelph Turfgrass Institute; Ted Leischner of Soil Foodweb Canada Ltd in Vulcan, AB; and Tim Livingstone and Jolly Farmer Products, Inc. of Northampton, NB.

Many thanks go to the editorial and production staff at Lone Pine Publishing for their hard work putting this book together, and special thanks to Shane Kennedy for his vision and faith in this project. I also thank the Creator.

Introduction

Growing an organic lawn is easy. However, your idea of what constitutes an ideal lawn might have to change. Some of the obstacles that prevent people from adopting organic practices include the lack of tolerance for weeds in their lawns, their wish to have a deep blue-green lawn and the mistaken belief that returning your grass clippings to the lawn (grasscycling) contributes to thatch buildup. In this age of instant gratification, people want immediate results without it costing them a fortune. People are also subjected to huge amounts of advertising by the chemical and fertilizer companies, who promise quick results at a reasonable cost. Many people are not aware of the alternatives. The intent of this book is to present alternatives to the current, chemical-dependent paradigm of lawn growing.

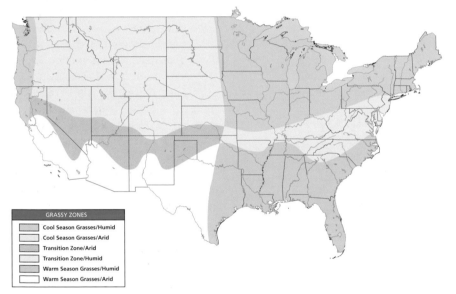

GRASSY ZONES

- Cool Season Grasses/Humid
- Cool Season Grasses/Arid
- Transition Zone/Arid
- Transition Zone/Humid
- Warm Season Grasses/Humid
- Warm Season Grasses/Arid

Home lawns comprise the vast majority of turfgrass grown, more than all the golf courses, sports fields and parks combined. We have the choice to be environmentally aware of everything we are doing with our lawns and to the environment, or to be environmentally ignorant and continue to blindly poison our environment. Something as simple as grasscycling, or composting your collected clippings, helps reduce the stress on the environment.

There has been a recent trend to reduce or eliminate lawns in the home landscape. This trend has been encouraged by the perception that lawn maintenance practices are bad for the environment. It is claimed that lawns waste water, the fertilizers used leach into the groundwater, the pesticides used for weeds and insects are toxic to our health and can leach into the groundwater, grass clippings are filling up landfills and lawns are too labor intensive. There is also a concern about disposal of empty pesticide containers. Some of these concerns are valid, but they can be reduced or eliminated by using the advice presented here.

It is easy to grow an organic lawn that could very well be the envy of the neighborhood. The information included in this book is for an average home lawn and deals with the most common species of turfgrasses used in the northern United States, including grass species for the transition zone.

The Benefits of Growing a Lawn

There are many good reasons for growing a lawn.

- Lawns benefit the environment.
- A healthy stand of turfgrass greatly reduces wind and water erosion.
- Lawns suck up carbon dioxide and ozone, and produce oxygen. An average lawn of approximately 2500 square feet will produce enough oxygen for a family of 4 people.
- Lawns trap dust and other particulate matter from the air, reducing the amount of dust and mud around homes and other buildings, and in the air we breathe.
- Lawns are very efficient at filtering water as it passes through the soil profile, protecting and even improving water quality. Lawns help water infiltrate into the soil, helping to reduce the amount of soil and contaminants that run off into our rivers and lakes.

- The soil foodweb under a healthy turfgrass lawn is efficient at degrading synthetic, organic chemical pollutants.
- Turfgrass can reduce noise levels by up to 40%, and because turfgrass reflects light in many directions, the glare from the sun is noticeably reduced.
- Lawns can help lower air conditioning costs by helping to keep the air cool. On a hot, sunny day, stand on a lawn and then stand in the middle of the street. You will experience a marked difference in the amount of heat in each location, with the temperature cooling the farther you move away from the street (or any paved area).
- A healthy, mowed lawn discourages some pests, such as mice, ticks and snakes, from making their home there.
- Healthy, mowed lawns help reduce the amount of pollen in the air by suppressing weed growth and by preventing plants from producing flowers.
- Turfgrass, the most durable groundcover plant available, provides a stable, cushioned surface to play sports and games on. A healthy, dense turfgrass helps reduce injuries from sports and other play activities.
- Aesthetically, a quality turfgrass lawn increases the property value and curb appeal of homes and businesses.

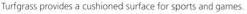
Turfgrass provides a cushioned surface for sports and games.

Enjoying a natural lawn

- Lawns provide a neutral space between flower and shrub beds.
- Turfgrass lawns provide security. It's easy to spot an intruder moving across a wide-open lawn. A healthy, mowed lawn also provides a fire break against wildfires.
- Lastly, well-maintained turfgrass offers us a place for relaxing and reconnecting with Mother Earth. Who has not enjoyed lying down on a cool, green lawn on a nice summer day?

The Turfgrass Plant

Following is a description of the basic parts of a turfgrass plant—the parts that are of most concern when growing and maintaining a lawn.

Turfgrass roots

Turfgrass plants have dense, fibrous root systems. Most of the turfgrass roots for cool-season turfgrasses that are cut at 2" will be in the top 5–6" of the soil. At a 3" mowing height, the roots more than double in volume and extend to an 8–9" depth, leading to stronger plants. Turfgrass roots grow best in soils with adequate water, air and nutrients.

Turfgrass roots live for 6 months to 2 years. Cool-season turfgrasses have the most root growth in spring and early summer, and often lose most of those roots during the heat of summer. Root growth is initiated again in fall when the temperature cools. Some species have roots that constantly die off and are replaced; these turfgrasses replace their root systems every year. Some other turfgrass species retain most of their root systems for more than one year.

Causes of poor root growth
- mowing too short or too often
- compacted, waterlogged or excessively warm soil
- soil with a pH below 5.0
- excessive nitrogen in the soil
- a lack of available potassium
- excessive thatch
- suppressed microbial activity (poor foodweb health)

Turfgrass shoots

Shoots are the stems and leaves of the turfgrass plant. Turfgrass shoots grow from a small area known as the crown, and from nodes on lateral shoots such as rhizomes and stolons (see Vegetative reproduction, p. 10). The turfgrass shoot has a short, very compressed stem, with leaves produced alternately (one above the other on opposite sides of the stem) from nodes on the stem.

Kentucky bluegrass

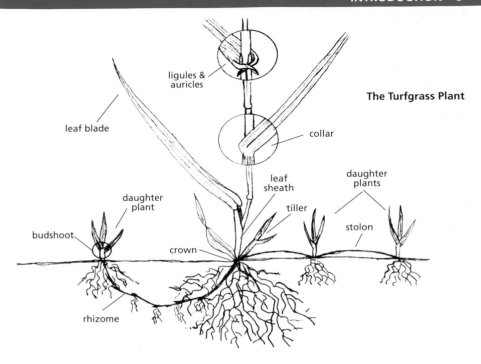

The Turfgrass Plant

ligules & auricles
leaf blade
collar
leaf sheath
daughter plants
daughter plant
tiller
stolon
budshoot
crown
rhizome

Turfgrass leaves

A turfgrass leaf consists of an upper, flattened, narrow blade and a lower, rounded, hollow leaf sheath that encircles the stem. Photosynthesis occurs in the leaves. Leaves have parallel veins, and the blades sometimes have a prominent midrib. The leaf features are the keys to identifying the turfgrasses in a lawn.

Leaf blades range in color from bright apple green to dark green to blue-green. In cross-section they can be flat, V-shaped or keeled, such as you would see on the bottom of a boat. Young blades are generally upright in growth; as the leaf matures, the blade takes on a more horizontal habit. The tips of the blades differ among the turfgrass species.

The base of the leaf sheath varies in color from white to reddish to purple. Each leaf sheath surrounds the sheaths of younger leaves and is surrounded by the sheaths of older leaves, and collectively this is called the budshoot. The arrangement of the new leaves is either folded or rolled in the budshoot.

In the area where the blade and the leaf sheath meet are the ligule, auricles and collar. The ligule is a structure that extends upward, often clasping the stem, and is located on the upper side of the leaf. These are membranous or hairy, and can be short and barely visible, prominent or absent altogether. The auricles are structures that grow outward from the sides of the collar. They can be short and stubby, long and grasping or absent. The collar divides the leaf sheath and leaf blade, and is seen as a band. It is located on the side of the leaf facing away from the stem. The band can be narrow or wide, and can stretch across the whole leaf or can be separated in the middle.

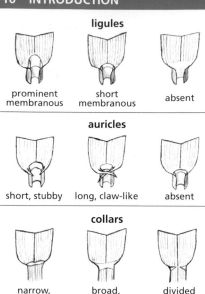

ligules

| prominent membranous | short membranous | absent |

auricles

| short, stubby | long, claw-like | absent |

collars

| narrow, continuous | broad, continuous | divided |

leaf arrangement in the budshoot

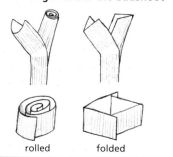

| rolled | folded |

The turfgrass crown

The crown is the life center of the turfgrass plant. It is from this area that new shoots and roots are borne. A turfgrass plant can lose all of its roots and leaves and still survive if the crown remains viable. It is also the area where the vascular systems of the roots and shoots join up. The crown is located at the base of the plant, at the soil line or very near to it.

Vegetative reproduction

Turfgrasses reproduce by seed and by vegetative means. Vegetative reproduction is the production of new turfgrass plants by methods other than seed, and it is these methods that we rely upon for growing our lawns. By mowing our lawns we prevent the turfgrass plants from reproducing from seed, with annual bluegrass being an exception. Vegetative reproduction comes in the form of tillers, rhizomes and stolons.

Turfgrass plants must reach a specific level of maturity before tillers, rhizomes or stolons are produced. Healthy plants with lots of leaves and energy reserves enhance tiller, rhizome and stolon development, as do the cool, moist days of spring and fall. Mowing the lawn stimulates the growth of tillers, rhizomes and stolons. Rhizomes and stolons are larger in diameter than turfgrass roots, and are able to effectively store carbohydrate energy reserves. When turfgrasses are injured, they have different recovery rates depending on the growth habit; grasses that have rhizomes or stolons will recover more quickly than bunch-type grasses.

Tillers are upright lateral shoots that branch off of the primary shoot just above the crown to form new plants. Tillers only live for a short time, and are constantly replaced by new tillers. Turfgrasses that only produce tillers form a bunch-type growth habit, as seen in perennial ryegrass and sheep fescue.

Rhizomes are underground lateral shoots that arise from the plant's crown. They grow relatively horizontally through the soil away from the plant, sending up the tip to form a new plant. New plants can also grow from each node on the rhizome, especially when the rhizome is cut or injured. The new plant will produce its own rhizomes once it matures. Rhizomes can produce branches, especially when they are injured. Kentucky bluegrass and creeping fescue spread by rhizomes.

Stolons are aboveground lateral shoots that arise from the crown and grow horizontally along the surface. New plants are easily produced from each node along the stolon. Verticutting stimulates rooting at the stolon nodes. Creeping and velvet bentgrass produce stolons.

It is important to know what method of vegetative reproduction your lawn grasses have, as that can affect the maintenance you provide. Maintenance preferences for each of the main turfgrass species are provided with the individual species information beginning on page 23.

More roots than shoots

When growing, turfgrass shoots depend on the roots for water and nutrients, while roots depend on the shoots for carbohydrates. Both roots and shoots need carbohydrates for proper growth. The best situation is for your turfgrass plants to have more roots than shoots. The conditions that favor shoot growth over root growth include low carbohydrate reserves, high temperatures above the optimum for good growth, a mowing height at or below the low end of the preferred height range, low light levels and high nitrogen levels.

Competition

Individual turfgrass plants require light, air, water and nutrients for their survival, but there is always competition for the available supply of these essentials. This competition can occur between plants of the same species or cultivars, and between different species and cultivars. Plants that have more seedling vigor and a bigger energy reserve in their seeds, plants that develop their roots faster, and plants that are more vigorous growers will out-compete weaker plants growing near them. In time, the stronger and better adapted plants in your lawn will come into balance so that each individual plant has all the light, air, water and nutrients it needs.

When seeding a lawn, different grass species or cultivars will compete in areas best suited for their growth. The turfgrass plants that are best adapted to your environment, soil type and situation are the plants that will succeed. For example, in a mixture of Kentucky bluegrass and red fescue, the Kentucky bluegrass will out-compete red fescue in sunny positions, and red fescue will out-compete Kentucky bluegrass in shadier spots. This process can take from one to four years.

Other considerations, such as uniformity, come to mind when selecting turfgrasses for your lawn. When putting together a blend or mixture of turfgrasses, ideally the constituent plants will have similar leaf texture, growth habit, color, shoot density and vertical growth rates. Such a mixture or blend provides your lawn with a uniform appearance, a feature that is important for showcase front lawns, but not as important for back lawns.

Turfgrass Environment

JUST AS WITH ANY OTHER PLANT OR ANIMAL, TURFGRASS NEEDS TO LIVE
under certain conditions—the turfgrass environment—to perform at its best.
This environment includes good soil conditions and the right amount of sunlight,
air and water. The turfgrass environment also includes the amount of traffic the
turfgrass experiences.

Lawn in full sun

Light

Cool-season turfgrasses prefer a minimum of 4–5 hours of sunlight per day,
and more if the lawn is heavily used.
When turfgrasses do not receive
enough sunlight, they become weak
and thin. Such lawns are more susceptible to disease, especially in cool,
moist, shady areas. Lawns in the shade
are more subject to erosion, which
increases the risk of sediments and
pollutants entering the water system.

Water

The infiltration rate, or how fast water
moves into your soil, is influenced by
the soil structure, soil texture, percolation rate and surface conditions such
as thatch or some form of crust.

The percolation rate is how fast the
water that has infiltrated into the soil
flows downward to the water table or
to a drainage tile. Percolation is influenced by the size, amount and conti-
nuity of the pore space, the presence
of water already in the rootzone and
the resistance encountered from
trapped air.

Turfgrass growing in soil that is
experiencing moderate water stress
will grow longer roots to seek water at
deeper soil levels. Turfgrass plants
growing in soil that is experiencing
a severe water deficit will have fewer,
shorter and more spindly leaves per
plant, a major loss of roots and a big
drop in plant vigor.

Shady location for a lawn

Wilt

Visually, wilt is seen as drooping leaves, rolling or folding of leaves or loss of turgidity. The usual first symptom is the foliage changing to a blue-gray color. Footprinting (see Watering, p. 64) occurs when a turfgrass is under wilt conditions.

Conditions that enhance wilt include high temperatures, wind, intense sunlight and low relative humidity. Wilt occurs more often on the tops of hills and on steep slopes, especially those that face south. Turfgrass with a thick thatch layer is prone to wilt.

Wet wilt occurs when there is poor uptake of water by the roots, or when there is a small or compromised root system that will not take up as much water as the plant requires. Wet wilt can occur regardless of how much moisture is in the soil. Root systems can be damaged after a severe moisture deficit stress or during lengthy rains or periods of high humidity, when lack of oxygen needed for respiration kills the roots' tiny root hairs. Poor rooting can also be caused or affected by compacted soil, root-feeding insects, root disease,

scalping, high soil salt levels and excessive quick-release nitrogen fertilizer.

Different turfgrass species have different tolerances to wilting. The fescues, especially the fine fescues, are the most tolerant of the conditions that cause wilt. Kentucky bluegrass is moderately wilt resistant. The bentgrasses and ryegrasses are the most susceptible to wilt.

Temporary wilt can cause injury or death of a turfgrass plant. An internal plant water deficit hinders the plant's metabolic processes. Intense sunlight can fry the foliage. Wilted turf is subject to mechanical damage from traffic, especially vehicle traffic.

Wilt can be prevented by proper watering and mowing, good soil aeration, balanced fertility (no quick-release nitrogen fertilizers) and keeping the thatch layer under control.

After periods of drought, dormant turfgrass may be healthier and better able to recover when conditions improve than turf that has been over-watered or underwatered during the drought conditions.

Lawns beside ponds and streams may be subject to flooding.

Floods

Flooding of turf can cause extensive damage, depending on how long the area remains flooded. Soil oxygen can be depleted in only a few hours and there is usually quite a mess to clean up afterward. Floodwater often has a huge amount of suspended silt and clay particles that can create a soil layer of a different texture on top of the existing soil, resulting in poor water and air infiltration.

The effects of flooding can be lessened by removing as much of the debris and deposited material as you are able to, rinsing as much of the soil particles and salts off the foliage as possible and core aerating to help open up the soil to air exchange.

Air

Like humans and animals, plants need to breathe. The soil needs good air exchange for plants to be healthy. Air movement (wind) helps keep the turfgrass cool by breaking up and mixing the air layer that develops over turfgrass in still air. Too much wind can cause desiccation, but a gentle wind increases plant transpiration, which has a cooling effect on the plant, similar to when we sweat and then stand in a light breeze. A gentle wind also helps with carbon dioxide (CO_2) exchange in the soil.

There can also be detrimental effects from wind. Stiff winds can blow sand and soil across the turf surface, which can shear off the grass blades. Wind can spread soil, seeds, pollen, snow and spores. Lawns near the coast are subject to salt spray; this spray should be rinsed off the foliage as part of your regular maintenance.

Air is drawn into the soil after watering. Although there is some oxygen dissolved in rain and irrigation water, the vast majority of oxygen must come from the atmosphere. Gravity pulls the water down into the soil, and this water movement creates somewhat of a vacuum in the pore space above the water, which draws air in behind it. Large pore space is critical for this process to occur. There must be gas exchange in the soil—oxygen must get in, while carbon dioxide and other toxic gasses must be released to the atmosphere. Waterlogged and compacted soils greatly limit air exchange.

Turfgrasses are better adapted to soils with low oxygen levels than many other plants, but still need a certain amount of oxygen for good health. It is best to eliminate waterlogged and compacted soils to allow the free flow of oxygen.

Soil

Physical properties

The physical properties of soil have a direct influence on the amount of pore space, on air and water infiltration and movement through the soil and on water retention. Pores are spaces between the organic and mineral components of the soil. Soils with good structure have a balance of large and small pores. It is through these pore spaces that air and water move in the soil.

The texture of the soil is determined by the percentages of sand, silt and clay in the soil. When there are two different, distinct textured soils sitting one on top of the other, such as sand over gravel, the difference in textures creates a boundary that 'perches' water in the upper level until it has reached saturation. Only when the top layer is totally saturated does water move into the lower layer.

Soil structure is the arrangement of the mineral and organic components into stable aggregates. The aggregation process is aided by roots pushing through the soil and from the substances the roots secrete, by wetting and drying, by freezing and thawing, and especially by soil microorganisms in their search for food.

The basic soil structures include single grain, granular or crumb, platy,

blocky, columnar, prismatic and massive. The appearances of the different soil structures are well described by their names. Single grain and granular (crumb) soil structures are the best for growing turfgrass. Straight sand has a single grain structure and loam usually has a granular- (crumb-) type structure. The other soil structure types need some amending or renovation to grow good-quality turfgrass. Intense traffic destroys soil structure.

Wet, soupy soil does not compact in the way that moist soil does, but the soil structure is more completely destroyed. Moist soil can pack together in a ball when you pick up a handful. Wet soil does not pack together at all, but rather will flow through your fingers when you pick up a handful.

Chemical properties

Cation exchange capacity (CEC) is the measure of the ability of a soil to retain nutrients in the form of cations (positively charged atoms or groups of

Granular (crumb) soil structure

Columnar soil structure

Good surface drainage requires that the ground have a minimum 1% slope away from buildings and toward drains.

Subsurface drainage is necessary when the soil lacks good internal drainage. A lack of internal drainage can be caused by poor aeration, compacted soil or clay soil. It is possible that, even though your topsoil drains well enough, it may be sitting on impenetrable clay that does not drain at all.

Drainage can be enhanced by improving the soil structure or by installing subsurface drainage. Structure can be improved by amending the soil with organic matter. Do not add sand to a clay soil, as 'concrete' may be the result.

Soil pore space

Coarse soils have large pore spaces; finer soils have fewer large pore spaces but more capillary spaces. Water and air move easily through large pores, whereas water is retained in the smaller pores. The smaller the pore size the more tightly the water is held in the soil.

Acidic soils

Soils tend to become acidic in areas where rainfall is plentiful, such as the Pacific Northwest, Pennsylvania, New York and the New England area. Soil pH affects nutrient availability, microorganism activity (neutral soil favors microbial activity) and the solubility of toxic elements. A slightly acidic soil pH of 6.5 has the highest availability of plant nutrients. Strongly acidic soils lead to greater thatch accumulation, poor soil structure, low earthworm populations, poor rooting, lower plant vigor and a reduction of drought tolerance.

atoms). Some soil components are able to absorb more cations than others. Clay and organic matter have the ability to absorb many cations (a high CEC) as compared to sand, which has a very low CEC.

Organic matter, such as compost, improves soil structure, aeration, water retention, water movement and nutrient availability.

Drainage

Drainage is a key factor for growing quality turfgrass. The soil must be able to drain so the turfgrass is not sitting in a pool of water. Waterlogged soils can cause shallow rooting, lack of vigor, poor health, poor aeration, increased disease incidents, risk of damage to soil structure and an increased likelihood of the soil being compacted. Wet soils also are slower to warm up in spring.

Liming soils corrects acidity

Acid soils lack calcium and magnesium, and phosphorous is tied up. Liming soils neutralizes acidic soil and can correct magnesium and calcium deficiencies, as lime is composed of calcium or calcium and magnesium. Lime also binds with aluminum and iron in the soil to form soluble compounds that leach from the soil. Aluminum can be toxic at low soil pH. Alkaline soils with high lime levels may lack the iron needed for healthy growth. Always apply lime, and any other amendment, based on a soil test and foodweb assay. Too much lime can be detrimental.

Light lime applications on heavily thatched turf can raise the pH of the thatch and stimulate soil microorganisms, which will help to remove the excess thatch.

Forms of lime

While calcitic limestone is mostly calcium and dolomitic limestone is composed of both calcium and magnesium, both forms have a long residual action and both are faster acting when finely ground. Oxides and hydroxides of calcium and magnesium are fast acting but require careful handling.

The best time to apply lime is late fall to early winter. The freeze/thaw action in the fall and spring helps incorporate the lime into the soil. Liming just before a rainfall is good too, as the rain washes the lime off the foliage and into the soil. The best time to apply any soil amendment (always based on a soil test) is when the amendments can be incorporated into the soil before seeding or sodding.

Alkaline soils

Alkaline soils are common in areas where rainfall is limited and the soils are not leached of excess salts. Soils with pH 7.5–8.4 can be detrimental to turfgrass growth. A good correction for alkaline soil is to apply elemental sulfur, which can be mixed with sand or topdressing for easier application. Do not apply sulfur during periods of summer turfgrass stress, such as heat and drought.

Saline and sodic soils

Saline and sodic soils occur in areas with arid, sunny conditions and where soil drainage is restricted, such as some areas of the Midwest and the Great Plains states. These areas lack good surface drainage and have low soil permeability.

Saline soils, which have a high salt/low sodium content, are often seen with a white crust. The source of this crust can be the irrigation water (test!), drainage water, groundwater from a high water table or the weathering of the soil parent material. Saline

Areas that experience lots of rain tend to have acidic soils.

soils can be amended if they can be properly drained. Excess salts can then be leached from the soil. Ensure the irrigation water has a low salt content. Water deeply to help flush the salts from the soil—light, frequent waterings are ineffective. Natural precipitation is good for leaching, provided that drainage is available.

Sodic soils have a pH greater than 8.4, a high sodium content and poor soil structure. Generally, these soils are not suitable for use as lawns. There are some grass species that have a higher tolerance for sodium in soils; these are generally used for low-maintenance areas such as roadside ditches and erosion control. Wheatgrasses have high tolerance for sodium in soils.

Soil modification

Turfgrasses can grow on most soils. However, without soil modification your maintenance regime will have to be modified for the available soil type. Lawns grown on heavier clay and silt soils require a much different maintenance than lawns grown on sandy soil. Soil modification is often done for soils with high clay or sand content, and for those areas that have high levels of lawn traffic.

When we modify soils for lawn growth we change the chemical, biological and physical properties of the rootzone. An ideal rootzone for turfgrass is one with minimal compaction tendencies (the main goal of renovations), good water infiltration and percolation rates, good aeration and a balance of large and small pore spaces for deep rooting, no toxic substances, a healthy soil foodweb, good cation exchange capacity and good water retention.

You should know the intended use for the area and why you are modifying the soil. The different soil amendment materials have different properties and thus different effects on soil texture, soil structure, chemical properties and biological properties. The amendments also have different long-term stability, availability and cost, another reason why soil tests are so important. Do not amend your soil without a soil test and a foodweb assay.

Traffic

Turfgrass traffic causes turfgrass wear, soil compaction and soil displacement (wet soils are particularly vulnerable). Heavy traffic can injure, thin or kill plants; direct pressure on the turfgrass plants crushes, scuffs and tears the leaves, crowns and stems. Traffic-injured turf is more susceptible to disease, which can enter through the wounds.

Wear tolerance

Different species of turfgrass have different wear tolerance—tough, coarse grasses tend to have higher wear tolerance than lush, soft grasses. For the grasses we grow as lawns, tall fescue has the best wear tolerance; perennial ryegrass has good tolerance; Kentucky bluegrass and red fescue have medium tolerance; and the bentgrasses have poor tolerance. There is also a difference in wear tolerance among cultivars of each species. Rhizomatous grasses recover quickly from wear damage. Young seedlings are not as wear tolerant as mature plants.

How you maintain your turfgrass will influence wear tolerance. Healthy, vigorous turf has better wear tolerance and recovers quicker from wear damage than weakened, stressed or dormant turf. Higher mowing height increases wear tolerance. A layer of

thatch 1/2" thick improves wear tolerance by providing cushioning from traffic. Excess fertility or any practice that causes lush, succulent growth decreases wear tolerance, whereas adequate potassium will improve wear tolerance. Nutrient-deficient turf is not wear tolerant.

Environment plays a role in wear tolerance. Lawns that have been overwatered, lawns in shade, lawns under wilt conditions and lawns in dormancy have poor wear tolerance. Frost-covered turf is susceptible to damage through the action of mechanical disruption of cells by ice crystals. Avoid, if possible, walking or driving on lawns that have frost, as the leaves and crown may be damaged. Lawns in the process of thawing after

Lawn showing mild wear and compaction damage

Lawns provide paths between plants, but the traffic can cause problems.

winter are also vulnerable to damage. When only the top layer of the area is thawed, it can slide over the frozen area underneath, shearing roots and rhizomes in the process. Dormant turf is most at risk during periods of minimal snow cover; during wet, slushy periods of freeze-thaw; and in locations with heavy winter traffic.

Soil compaction

Soil compaction is another result of turfgrass use and wear. We have all seen the effects of heavy traffic on turfgrass. Think of a path worn into the grass where people have created a shortcut, or the area in front of soccer goalposts as seen in many of our schoolyards. Compaction—the pressing together of the soil particles into a denser soil

mass—is caused by foot and vehicle traffic, rain or irrigation droplets (especially on bare soil), and heavy equipment used in the original construction of the area. The heaviest compaction occurs in the top 2–3" of the soil surface, with the top inch being the most compacted.

Compaction causes the destruction of the soil structure. It reduces the amount of large and small pore spaces in the soil. In compacted soils, toxic gasses can build up in the rootzone, infiltration and percolation of water is reduced and surface runoff is increased. Compacted soils are effective in preventing roots from penetrating through the soil.

Soil compaction is influenced by the soil texture (sand, silt, clay, organic matter), the soil water content, the severity and frequency of pressure applied to the soil and the amount of plant cover. Clay soils, the easiest soils to compact, often create flat, horizontal, overlapping plates that severely restrict water and air movement in the soil. Sand compacts much less than clay. Golf course greens and tees, and sports fields use 60–85% screened sand in the rootzone to improve compaction resistance. The more water a soil has, up to a point, the more easily it is compacted. Waterlogged soils do not compact, but the soil structure is easily destroyed. Spring is when most soil compaction occurs, as this is when the soil is usually the wettest. One bonus for us is that freezing and thawing in the spring helps alleviate compacted soil. For areas that have constant traffic, it may be better to replace the soil with an alternate surface, such as a raised or paved path.

Lawn with severe wear and compaction damage

Soil displacement
Soil displacement is caused by constant light traffic, which exposes the soil so that it can then be moved away by wind, water and further traffic, and by heavy traffic, especially on overly moist and wet soils. Heavy traffic damage often occurs when people back a vehicle onto a lawn when moving household items. This type of damage can be alleviated by using planks to distribute the vehicle's weight more evenly.

Typical traffic damage on a soccer field

The Turfgrass Species

THE QUALITY OF YOUR LAWN DEPENDS ON THE SPECIES OF GRASS USED, the level of maintenance, the environmental conditions including type of soil, and the planned usage of the turfgrass (front lawn, back lawn, play area, etc.). Each species or cultivar of turfgrass has different properties that make it more or less suitable for each desired use. These properties include differing levels of disease and insect tolerance, wear tolerance, recuperative potential and environmental tolerance (shade, drought, etc.). For a quality lawn, it is important to choose the species or cultivar that has the properties needed for the intended use. You should also attempt to have a diversity of turfgrass species and cultivars in your lawn. Diversity helps control the severity of pest outbreaks.

Kentucky bluegrass–fescue lawn

The turfgrasses we use for our lawns in the northern US (see Grassy Zones map, p. 6) are known as cool-season turfgrasses. The main cool-season turfgrasses are Kentucky bluegrass, creeping red fescue, chewings fescue and perennial ryegrass. Gaining in popularity and use for lawns is turf-type tall fescue. These turfgrasses can all form a good, dense, high-quality lawn. Bentgrasses are included in the following list as these are sometimes used for home lawns. Warm-season turfgrasses are those species that grow well in the southern United States.

Cool-season turfgrasses begin to break winter dormancy as the soil begins to warm and the roots begin to grow. Active plant growth begins when the soil warms to 55° F. Root growth occurs before the shoots. Cool-season grasses grow most vigorously in spring and fall, the seasons when the temperature and moisture levels are most suitable for these turfgrasses. Optimal temperatures for cool-season turfgrasses are air temperatures of 60–75° F and soil temperatures of 50–65° F. As the heat of summer approaches, the plants slow their growth and enter summer dormancy if not watered regularly. When turfgrass plants are coming out of a period of summer or winter dormancy, new shoots grow from the crown and from the nodes on rhizomes and stolons. Cool-season grasses will grow until the soil freezes.

Warm-season turfgrasses grow vigorously during the heat of the summer months. The optimal temperatures for growth are soil temperatures of 70–90° F, and air temperatures of 80–95° F. Warm-season turfgrasses are usually lower growing and have deeper roots than cool-season species. Also, warm-season turfgrasses are generally more tolerant of heat, drought and wear than their cool-season counterparts. Warm-season turfgrasses go dormant when the temperatures cool in fall and the soil temperature drops to 50° F. The biggest factor that affects where warm-season turfgrasses will grow is the low temperature in winter. Cool-season grasses can handle the heat better than warm-season grasses can handle the cold.

There is an area known as the transition zone, which is the area where it is too hot in the summer for cool-season grasses, and too cold in the winter for warm-season grasses. Cool-season grasses are most often used in the transition zone, and tall fescue thrives in this zone. Some warm-season turfgrasses are also used in the transition zone. Zoysiagrass will also grow well in the transition zone, especially the newer cultivars that are more cold-tolerant. Bermuda grass is best in the Deep South and in the southern portions of the transition zone.

There has been, and continues to be, a great deal of research in the development of turfgrass cultivars. Good cultivars are available for all the main turfgrasses listed in this book, and for some of the other turfgrasses and low-maintenance grasses also listed. Many new cultivars exhibit significantly greater shoot density, excellent disease resistance, improved tolerance to heat and drought stress, reduced thatch accumulation, and provide uniform non-grainy surfaces, finer leaf texture, more erect crown growth and a darker green color.

COOL-SEASON GRASSES

Kentucky Bluegrass
Poa pratensis

ID features
- Blade: medium to dark green or blue-green; keeled, V-shaped to flat in cross-section; parallel sides; boat-shaped tip
- Sheath: white at base; folded in the budshoot
- Ligule: short, membranous, flat across the top
- Auricles: none

Kentucky bluegrass is a hardy, medium-textured, rhizomatous perennial, and is the most widely used cool-season turfgrass species. When injury takes place it heals rapidly because of its aggressive rhizomes. It greens up early in spring and retains its color well into fall. However, it tends to become dormant in summer, especially when the temperature is hot.

Kentucky bluegrass

Kentucky bluegrass lawn

Growing
Kentucky bluegrass performs well in full sun in well-drained, moist, fertile, slightly acidic soil. Kentucky bluegrass can tolerate waterlogged conditions for short periods. It is mostly grown from seed and spreads aggressively by rhizomes. The seeds germinate in about 21 days.

Use
Kentucky bluegrass is a good general-purpose turfgrass for most of the areas covered by this book, other than the coastal areas of the Pacific Northwest. It is used for home and business lawns, parks, cemeteries, sports fields, golf courses, in highway ditches for stability (providing a place for emergency stopping should the need arise) and at airports where some of the landing strips are turfgrass.

Kentucky bluegrass is useful when fast recovery is needed, such as on sports fields. It makes great, tightly knit sod owing to its rhizomes. Kentucky bluegrass mixes well with creeping red fescue and chewings fescue.

Maintenance
Kentucky bluegrass requires a medium-maintenance regime. Maintain a normal cutting height of 2–3". Dwarf cultivars are available that can be mowed at a height of 1–2", but hardiness is questionable in some parts of the country. Kentucky bluegrass requires regular water for the best performance, and will enter summer dormancy with a lack of irrigation. It requires $1/2$–1 lb of nitrogen per 1000 ft^2 per growing month.

Disease
Kentucky bluegrass is most susceptible to *Helminthosporium* blight. Other possible diseases include *Fusarium* blight, *Fusarium* patch, powdery mildew, *Pythium* blight, dollar spot, brown patch, *Ophiobolos* patch, *Typhula* blight, rust and striped smut.

Annual Bluegrass
Poa annua var. annua and P. annua var. reptans

Annual bluegrass is often referred to as a weed in turfgrass lawns. It is included here because it is sometimes encouraged to be the dominant species in a lawn

Turfgrass plants need a certain amount of nutrients, including nitrogen, for every month they are growing. Since nitrogen is the nutrient turfgrasses use the most and is water-soluble and mobile in the soil (it can leach out below the rootzone), it is used for noting turfgrass nutritional requirements. The nitrogen amount listed for each turfgrass helps illustrate the difference in nutritional requirements among the different turfgrasses in this book. Of course, turfgrasses need many more nutrients than nitrogen. If your soil is unable to provide the amount of nitrogen the plants need, it will have to be provided as part of the maintenance of your lawn. A healthy lawn with a fully functional foodweb will supply all the nutrients the turfgrass plants need (see Turfgrass Nutrition on page 84).

when environmental conditions favor its growth over other turfgrasses.

ID features

- Blade: apple green, narrow, V-shaped in cross-section, parallel sides that are sometimes puckered, boat-shaped tip
- Sheath: compressed, white at base, folded in the budshoot
- Ligule: prominent, membranous, white, pointed appearance
- Auricles: none

Poa annua var. *annua* is a low-growing, annual, bunch-type grass. *Poa annua* var. *reptans* (sometimes called *P. reptans*) is a weakly stoloniferous grass that has more shoots, tillers and roots than var. *annua*, but produces less seed. Annual bluegrasses are often considered weeds in other turfgrasses because their color and patchy growth habit disrupts uniformity. Also, annual bluegrass can be injured and thinned out because of its intolerance of temperature extremes and drought. Annual bluegrass can make a high-quality lawn when grown on its own. It does not recover well from injury, but can regenerate quickly from the seed bank in the soil.

Growing

Annual bluegrass grows well in full sun to part shade in moist, fertile, fine-textured, slightly acidic soils with high levels of phosphorous. It does very well in compacted, overwatered soils with poor drainage. It does not tolerate heat, cold or drought. Annual bluegrass produces seeds prolifically, even when mowed at a short height. It competes with bentgrasses under high-maintenance regimes, and with other turfgrasses when they are mowed too short. It invades lawns easily and it is difficult to control. Seed for *P. a.* var. *reptans* is available.

Use

Annual bluegrass is not planted as a home lawn. It is, however, present in many lawns and can either be encouraged or discouraged to grow depending on your maintenance. It has some use in areas with heavy traffic and compacted areas where no other grass will grow.

Maintenance

To encourage annual bluegrass, lower your mowing height to under ¾". Annual bluegrasses can be mowed as low as ¼". Irrigate frequently and shallowly, and provide a high level of fertility, up to 1 lb of nitrogen per 1000 ft^2 per growing month. Thatch can build quickly under these conditions. Do not collect the clippings when the plant is producing seeds.

To discourage annual bluegrass, relieve compacted soils by core aerating and topdressing, and aerate before or after seed production occurs. Irrigate deeply and infrequently. Raise the mowing height well above $^3/_4$", and collect grass clippings when annual bluegrass is in seed. Use a natural, pre-emergent herbicide, such as corn gluten, to reduce seed germination in the spring. Do not overuse fertilizers.

Disease

Annual bluegrass is susceptible to *Helminthosporium* species, *Fusarium* blight, *Fusarium* patch, *Pythium* blight, red thread, dollar spot, brown patch, *Ophiobolos* patch, *Typhula* blight and striped smut.

Creeping Red Fescue
Festuca rubra

ID features

- Blade: medium to dark green or blue-green, narrow, stiff, acute tip
- Sheath: round, reddish at base; folded in the budshoot

Creeping red fescue

- Ligule: short, membranous, flat across the top
- Auricles: none

Creeping red fescue is a hardy, fine-textured, bunch-type turfgrass with a dense, fibrous root system that spreads by tillers and short rhizomes. The rhizomes are not as aggressive or extensive as those on Kentucky bluegrass. Chewings fescue and sheep fescues do not have creeping red fescue's creeping growth habit. Creeping red fescue has good resistance to wear, but poor recuperative potential. The leaf blades grow slower than other turfgrasses in full sun. They grow faster than other species in shade, but the turf density will be less than when grown in full sun.

Growing
Creeping red fescue grows well in sun or partial shade in well-drained soil and it adapts well to sandy and acid soils. It does poorly in wet, poorly drained soils and in soils with high salt levels. It is very drought resistant once established, with a much lower water need than other turfgrasses—it rolls its leaves inward to conserve water in dry conditions. It is grown from seed and the seeds germinate in about 14 days.

Use
Creeping red fescue will produce an excellent stand of turfgrass on its own and it mixes very well with Kentucky bluegrass. It has the same uses as Kentucky bluegrass and it is excellent for erosion control and soil stabilization because of its dense root system.

Maintenance
Creeping red fescue requires a low- to medium-maintenance regime. It should be mowed in the range of 2–3", but it can be mowed as low as 1" and still form a dense lawn. It requires only 0.2–0.5 lb of nitrogen per 1000 ft^2 per growing month, and prefers low amounts of irrigation. Too much water or too much fertility will cause this turfgrass to decline in quality, as well as increase the potential for disease development.

Disease
Creeping red fescue is most susceptible to *Helminthosporium* blight. Other possible diseases include red thread, *Fusarium* patch, powdery mildew, *Pythium* blight, dollar spot, *Ophiobolos* patch and *Typhula* blight.

Chewings Fescue
Festuca rubra var. commutata

ID features
- Blade: medium green to blue-green, upright, narrow, stiff, acuminate tip
- Sheath: round, reddish at base; folded in the budshoot
- Ligule: short, membranous, flat across the top
- Auricles: none

Chewings fescue is a hardy, fine-textured, bunch-type turfgrass with a dense, fibrous root system. It spreads by tillers. It has better shade and wear tolerance than creeping red fescue, but also has poor recuperative potential.

The leaf blades grow slower than other turfgrasses in full sun, but faster than other species in the shade, though the turf density will be less than when grown in full sun. The newer cultivars have had the clumping habit bred out of them, improving their performance as turfgrasses.

Growing
Chewings fescue grows well in sun or partial shade in well-drained soil. It adapts well to sandy and acid soils, and is quite tolerant of infertile soils. It will do poorly in wet, poorly drained soils and in soils with high salt levels. It is very drought resistant once established, with a much lower water need than other turfgrasses. In dry conditions it rolls its leaves inward to conserve water. It is grown from seed, and the seeds germinate in about 14 days.

Use
Chewings fescue is often mixed with Kentucky bluegrass and/or creeping red fescue. It can be used on its own, but the bunch-type habit will form a clumpy lawn if not maintained for good health.

Maintenance
Chewings fescue requires a low- to medium-maintenance regime. Mowing should be in the range of 2–3", but it can be mowed as low as 1" and still form a dense lawn. It requires only 0.2–0.5 lb of nitrogen per 1000 ft^2 per growing month, and prefers low amounts of irrigation. Too much water or too much fertility will cause this turfgrass to decline in quality as well as increase the potential for disease development. It is less tolerant of excess water and fertility than creeping red fescue.

Disease
Chewings fescue is most susceptible to *Helminthosporium* blight. Other possible diseases include red thread, *Fusarium* patch, powdery mildew, *Pythium* blight, dollar spot, *Ophiobolos* patch and *Typhula* blight.

Perennial Ryegrass
Lolium perenne

ID features
- Blade: light yellow-green to medium green, shiny leaf backside, flat and keeled in cross-section, prominent midrib, acute tip
- Sheath: somewhat compressed, red/purple at base, folded in the bud-shoot
- Ligule: short to prominent, membranous, flat across the top
- Auricles: short, stubby, soft

Perennial ryegrass is a medium-textured, bunch-type turfgrass that

Chewings fescue

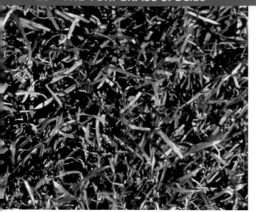

Perennial ryegrass

spreads by tillers. It has fair winter hardiness, and grows well in cool, moist climates. It is treated as an annual grass in the colder Northern, Midwest and Plains states. It has great wear tolerance, but has poor recovery potential from injury. The seed germinates rapidly (7 days, or less in ideal conditions), and is very aggressive during establishment. Be sure to select turf-type cultivars for use in your lawn because these have had some of the clumping habit bred out of them. Cultivars have also been developed that are slower growing vertically, darker green and easier to mow, making them more compatible with Kentucky bluegrass and other turfgrasses.

Growing

Perennial ryegrass grows best in full sun to partial shade in moist, fertile, well-drained soil, but can adapt to a wide range of soils. It is best adapted to areas with mild winters and cool, moist summers. It can be short lived in areas that experience temperature extremes. It is not tolerant of drought, but is tolerant of flooded conditions for short periods.

Use

Perennial ryegrass is used for home and business lawns, parks, cemeteries, sports fields, golf courses, in highway ditches for stability (providing a place for emergency stopping should the need arise) and at airports where some of the landing strips are turfgrass. It is mixed with fescue in the Pacific Northwest, and with Kentucky bluegrass in the Northeast and Midwest states. It is used on slopes where quick germination and growth are required and it is often used as a quick cover crop for severely damaged areas. It is used as a nurse grass in cold areas where it is not winter hardy. Nurse grasses protect the desirable species in a seed mixture. Perennial ryegrass can be quite aggressive—do not include more than 25% in any seed mix when used as a nurse grass; 5–10% in a mix is often plenty for flat ground. On steep slopes the percentage can be bumped up.

Maintenance

Perennial ryegrass requires a medium-maintenance regime. It can become clumpy when not maintained for aggressiveness. Maintain a normal cutting height of 2–3". Mower blades must be kept sharp when cutting ryegrass. Ryegrass leaf blades have a high number of very fibrous vascular bundles (grass veins and arteries) that are quite tough, and the cut tips of the grass can shred easily when cut with a dull mower. It has high water needs, and a nitrogen requirement of 0.4-0.8 lb of nitrogen per 1000 ft^2 per growing month.

Diseases

Helminthosporium species, *Fusarium* patch, *Pythium* blight, dollar spot, brown patch, *Typhula* blight, red thread, rust and striped smut may affect perennial ryegrass.

Perennial ryegrass lawn

Tall Fescue and Turf-type Tall Fescue
Festuca arundinacea

ID features
- Blade: dark green, flat in cross-section, keeled, stiff, prominent veins on upper leaf surface and prominent midrib beneath, acuminate tip
- Sheath: round, reddish at the base; rolled in the budshoot
- Ligule: short, wide, membranous, flat across the top
- Auricles: small, narrow, somewhat hairy

Tall fescue is an erect, bunch-type, medium- to coarse-textured perennial grass with a deep, extensive root system. It produces short rhizomes, but spreads mainly by tillers. Tall fescues have good insect and disease tolerance. They have excellent wear tolerance and will remain green through most summers without extra irrigation. Turf-type tall fescues have been selected and bred for lower growth habit, increased shoot density, darker green color and better shade and disease tolerance. Turf-type tall fescues have finer textured blades, and are a far better selection for home lawns than older varieties of tall fescue.

Growing
Tall fescue and turf-type tall fescue grow well in full sun to partial shade in moist, fertile, well-drained, slightly acidic, fine-textured soil, but can adapt to a wide range of soil and climatic conditions. They tolerate drought, alkaline and saline soils (with irrigation), soils of low fertility and wet soils. They are more heat tolerant than other cool-season turfgrasses, but low temperatures can be stressful and can cause lawns to become thin. Young seedlings are not cold tolerant and are prone to winterkill. Lawns may require over-seeding on a regular basis to maintain good quality. Some turf-type cultivars have improved cold weather tolerance. It is suggested to use at least 70% tall fescue or turf-type tall fescue seed, by weight, in seed mixtures. The seeds germinate rapidly.

Use
Turf-type tall fescues are used for lawns, playgrounds and sports fields, especially in hot, dry areas and areas with heavy traffic. Tall fescues are used for low-maintenance lawns, in highway

Turf-type tall fescue

Endophyte-enhanced turfgrasses

Turfgrasses have been developed that have been enhanced with endophytes. Endophytes are naturally occurring fungal organisms that live in symbiotic relationship with some species of turfgrasses, including perennial ryegrass, tall fescue and the fine fescues. Endophyte-enhanced turfgrasses have had endophytes artificially introduced to the plant. Turfgrasses with endophytes have been shown to repel surface-feeding insects like chinch bugs, billbugs, army worms and sod webworms, but are not effective against white grubs and other root feeders. They repel the insects by producing toxic compounds that deter insect feeding, but do not harm the plant.

Do not use endophyte-enhanced grasses anywhere animals are likely to graze. The toxic compounds can injure horses, cattle, sheep and other animals that feed on fresh or dried grass. These animals can suffer from delirium and livestock 'staggers,' as well as loss of appetite, rapid breathing, high body temperature, 'fescue foot' (which may result in the loss of hooves) and even death.

ditches, as airport landing strips and in watercourses, as they can tolerate being submerged. Tall fescues and turf-type tall fescues are very effective at erosion control and soil stabilization on banks.

Maintenance

Tall fescue requires a low- to medium-maintenance regime. It does not tolerate repeated mowing. Turf-type tall fescue performs well with a medium-maintenance regime. Maintain a normal cutting height of 2–3" for both. Although both tall fescues and turf-type tall fescues are drought tolerant, they perform well with regular water and good fertility of 0.4–1 lb of nitrogen per 1000 ft^2 per growing month.

Disease

Tall fescue is susceptible to *Fusarium* blight, especially in young lawns, *Ophiobolos* patch, *Typhula* blight and brown patch. It is somewhat resistant to *Helminthosporium* blight and rust.

Creeping Bentgrass
Agrostis palustris

ID features
- Blade: yellow green to medium green to blue green, flat in cross-section, narrow, acuminate tip
- Sheath: round, white at base; rolled in the budshoot
- Ligule: prominent, membranous, acute to oblong and may be notched
- Auricles: none

Creeping bentgrass is a very winter hardy, low-growing, fine-textured grass with fibrous, shallow roots. It spreads by stolons. It requires high levels of maintenance and can be very expensive to care for. It has poor resistance to disease and poor drought tolerance. Wear tolerance is poor to medium, but it improves with high maintenance, and the grass recovers fairly quickly from injury. It is slower to green up in spring and loses its color sooner in fall than Kentucky bluegrass and the red fescues.

Growing

Creeping bentgrass grows best in full sun in well-drained, moist, fertile, slightly acidic soil. Creeping bentgrass tolerates flooding and saline soils better than other cool-season turfgrasses,

Creeping bentgrass, colonial bentgrass and velvet bentgrass are susceptible to damage from common herbicides.

Creeping bentgrass lawn

but does not tolerate compacted soils. It is most often grown from seed, but is also grown using pieces of the stolons for sprigging and plugging. Seeds germinate in 7–14 days.

Use

Creeping bentgrass is best used for golf greens, tees and fairways, lawn bowling greens, tennis courts and croquet lawns. Bentgrasses are well adapted for lawns west of the Cascades in the Pacific Northwest, and do well in the Northeast, but can also be grown successfully anywhere you are prepared to provide a high level of maintenance. Bentgrasses are often used as mono-stands, as they are incompatible with many other turfgrass species, including all those listed above.

Maintenance

Mowing heights range from $3/16$–$5/8$". It develops a puffy growth habit and accumulates thatch quickly when mowed at the upper height range. It is easily scalped at higher mowing

heights. Regular vertical mowing will help control the thatch and stimulate rooting at the stolon nodes. Regular, light topdressing will also be required. Creeping bentgrass requires regular irrigation because of the shallow roots caused by the low cutting heights. It does not go dormant in the summer, but hot, dry conditions can severely injure the roots and restrict leaf growth. Bentgrass has a nitrogen requirement of 0.4–1 lb of nitrogen per 1000 ft^2 per growing month.

Disease

Creeping bentgrass is susceptible to a number of diseases including *Helminthosporium* species, *Fusarium* blight, *Fusarium* patch, *Pythium* blight, dollar spot, brown patch, red thread, *Typhula* blight and striped smut. Because of the susceptibility of bent-grasses to disease, preventative measures are often taken before the outbreak of disease. Fungicides can be used, but spraying compost tea has been shown to be very effective in preventing the outbreak of disease.

Colonial Bentgrass
Agrostis tenuis

ID features

- Blade: yellow green to medium green, flat in cross-section, erect, narrow, acuminate tip
- Sheath: round, white at base; rolled in the budshoot
- Ligule: short to prominent, membranous, flat across the top
- Auricles: none

Colonial bentgrass is a hardy, low-growing, fine-textured, bunch-type grass with fibrous, shallow roots. It can spread slowly by short stolons or rhizomes, if stolons or rhizomes are present. It is less tolerant to traffic and other turfgrass

Colonial bentgrass

buildup. Colonial bentgrass has moderate water needs, less than creeping bentgrass. It requires only 0.2–0.4 lb of nitrogen per 1000 ft² per growing month. It may need more fertility depending on the level of use.

Disease
Colonial bentgrass is susceptible to a number of diseases including *Helminthosporium* species, *Fusarium* patch, *Pythium* blight, *Ophiobolos* patch, dollar spot, brown patch, red thread, *Typhula* blight and striped smut.

Velvet Bentgrass
Agrostis canina

ID features
- Blade: bright green, flat in cross-section, narrow, acuminate tip
- Sheath: round, white at base; rolled in the budshoot
- Ligule: short, membranous, acute to oblong
- Auricles: none

Velvet bentgrass is a hardy, low-growing, soft, fine-textured, stoloniferous turfgrass that forms an attractive, dense lawn. It spreads more aggressively than colonial bentgrass, but not as quickly as creeping bentgrass. It is less tolerant to traffic and other turfgrass stresses than creeping bentgrass. The recovery potential when injured is poor to medium.

Growing
Velvet bentgrass grows well in full sun to part shade in well-drained, acidic soil of low to medium fertility. It is well adapted to cool, moist maritime climates, but has a low tolerance for hot, dry areas. It does not tolerate poorly drained, finely textured soils. It is grown from seed or from stolons. Velvet bentgrass is susceptible to iron chlorosis.

stresses than creeping bentgrass. The recovery potential when injured is poor to medium.

Growing
Colonial bentgrass grows well in full sun in well-drained, moist, fertile, slightly acidic soil. It needs regular water, as it does not tolerate heat or drought. It is grown from seed.

Use
Colonial bentgrass has the same uses as creeping bentgrass. Monostands of colonial bentgrass tend to be patchy after a few years, as variation exists in growth habit and color within the species.

Maintenance
Mowing heights range from ¼–¾". Colonial bentgrass develops a puffy growth habit and accumulates thatch quickly when mowed at the upper height range. It is easily scalped at higher heights of mowing. Light topdressing may be required to help control thatch

Use

Velvet bentgrass has the same uses as creeping bentgrass. Velvet bentgrass is best used for golf greens, tees and fairways, lawn bowling greens, tennis courts and croquet lawns. Bentgrasses are well adapted for lawns in the Pacific Northwest, and do well in the Northeast, but can also be grown successfully anywhere you are prepared to provide a high level of maintenance. Bentgrasses are often used as monostands, as they are incompatible with many other turfgrass species, including all the non-bentgrass species listed here.

Maintenance

Mowing heights range from $\frac{3}{16}$–$\frac{1}{2}$". Velvet bentgrass can develop thatch quickly. Regular vertical mowing will help control the thatch and stimulate rooting at the stolon nodes. Regular, light topdressing will also be required to help control thatch buildup. Velvet bentgrass has low to moderate water needs. It requires only 0.2–0.4 lb of nitrogen per 1000 ft^2 per growing month. It may need more fertility depending on the level of use.

Disease

Velvet bentgrass is susceptible to *Helminthosporium* species, *Fusarium* patch, *Pythium* blight, *Ophiobolos* patch, copper spot, brown patch, red thread and *Typhula* blight, but has good resistance to dollar spot.

The bentgrasses are all high-maintenance turfgrasses. They are low growing and not compatible with many other turfgrasses. You will need to use a good-quality reel mower that can cut within the desired height range, which is substantially lower than the 2–3" suggested for the non-bentgrass species listed.

Bentgrass lawns require high maintenance.

WARM-SEASON GRASSES

Zoysiagrass
Japanese Lawn Grass
Zoysia japonica

ID features
- Blade: variable from fine to coarse textured, dark green, flat in cross-section, stiff and somewhat wiry, sharply pointed tip
- Sheath: round to somewhat compressed, rolled in the budshoot
- Ligule: a short fringe of hairs
- Auricles: none

Zoysiagrass is a low-growing, heat-tolerant, perennial turfgrass that spreads by stolons and rhizomes. It forms a dense lawn that doesn't allow many weed species the room to grow. It has great wear tolerance, but is slow to recover from damage. Zoysiagrass lawns are often grown from sod, sprigs or plugs, but good-quality seeded

Zoysiagrass

Use

Zoysiagrass is used for home and business lawns, parks, sports fields and golf courses. It does not mix well with the cool-season grasses. Zoysiagrass grows well in the transition zone and south. Zoysiagrass is quite salt tolerant, and is used in coastal areas where there is good drainage.

Maintenance

Zoysiagrass requires a medium-maintenance regime. Maintain a normal cutting height of $1/2$–1". Mowing higher can result in puffy turf that is prone to scalping. Mower blades must be kept sharp. Zoysiagrass has wiry stems that quickly dull mower blades. It is a good idea to sharpen the blades a couple of times during the growing season. It has moderate water needs, and a nitrogen requirement of 0.4–1.0 lb of nitrogen per 1000 ft^2 per growing month.

Zoysiagrass requires a minimum of $1/2$" of water per week during periods of severe drought to keep the plants alive. Zoysiagrass also needs occasional watering during dry winters to prevent the plants from drying out.

Allow the grass to grow a little longer in the fall, as this provides insulation for the crowns during winter. Begin mowing in spring after the danger of a hard frost has passed and while the grass remains dormant. Zoysiagrass lawns tend to build up a thatch layer and verticutting may be necessary. Ensure you monitor this yearly. A healthy soil foodweb will help keep thatch at a minimum.

Diseases

Brown patch, rust, dollar spot and *Helminthosporium* leaf spot.

varieties are becoming more available. It is best to use plugs when planting into existing lawns or into weedy areas. Zoysiagrass is slow to establish, and it may creep into adjoining lawns and gardens.

Zoysiagrass goes dormant after the first frost, turning a light brown to straw color. It greens up in spring when soil temperatures rise above 60° F. For northern areas this may mean looking at a dormant lawn for six months. Select varieties that have a higher tolerance to cold. The wear tolerance is very low during winter dormancy.

Growing

Zoysiagrass grows well in **full sun**. Zoysiagrass tolerates more shade as you go south. The soil should be **well drained** and of **average fertility**, but zoysiagrass tolerates a wide range of soil types as long as they are well drained. Zoysiagrass tolerates heat and drought, but does best with regular moisture. The seeds germinate in about 10–14 days. Seeding rate is 2–3 lbs/1000 ft^2.

Bermuda Grass
Cynodon dactylon

ID features
- Blade: light to dark green, flat in cross-section, tapered sides, acute tip
- Sheath: compressed; folded in the budshoot
- Ligule: a short fringe of white hairs
- Auricles: none

Bermuda grass is a vigorous, low-growing, heat-tolerant, drought-tolerant, perennial turfgrass that spreads by stolons and rhizomes. It forms a dense lawn that competes well with weeds. It has great wear tolerance, and is quick to recover from damage. Wear damage on dormant turf recovers quickly in spring when growth resumes. Bermuda grass lawns are often grown from sod, sprigs or plugs, but good-quality seeded varieties are available. Bermuda grass is quick to establish and a fast grower, and will creep into adjoining lawns and gardens.

Bermuda grass goes dormant when soil temperatures drop below 55° F, and green up in spring when soil temperatures rise above the 55° F. Select varieties that have a higher tolerance to cold. In the southern transition zone and south, dormant Bermuda grass is often overseeded with perennial ryegrass or other cool-season grasses for winter color and use.

Growing
Bermuda grass grows best in **full sun** in **moist, fine-textured, well-drained, fertile** soil. Bermuda grass will adapt to a wide range of soil types. Bermuda grass is tolerant of floods and is salt tolerant, making it good for use in coastal areas. The seeds germinate in about 7–15 days. Seeding rate is 1–1$\frac{1}{2}$ lbs/1000 ft^2.

Use
Bermuda grass grows well in the southern part of the transition zone and south. Bermuda grass is used for a wide variety of lawn applications including home and business lawns, parks, sports fields and golf courses. It is sometimes mixed with tall fescue for home and business lawns.

Maintenance
Bermuda grass requires a medium- to high- maintenance regime. Maintain a normal cutting height of $\frac{1}{2}$–1". Bermuda grass looks best when mowed fairly frequently. Mowing higher can result in puffy turf that is prone to scalping. It prefers regular water, and has a nitrogen requirement of 0.8–1.8 lbs of nitrogen per 1000 ft^2 per growing month.

As with zoysiagrass lawns, Bermuda grass lawns tend to build up a thatch layer, and verticutting and topdressing with good-quality compost will often be necessary.

Diseases
Brown patch, rust, dollar spot, *Fusarium* patch, *Pythium* blight and *Helminthosporium* leaf spot.

Bermuda grass

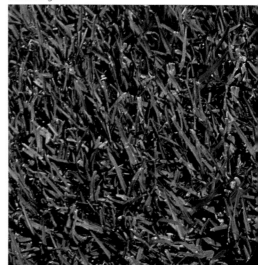

Lawn Installation

THIS SECTION IS FOR THOSE PEOPLE WHO ARE INSTALLING A NEW LAWN or re-establishing an old one. Installing a lawn requires physical and mental effort, beginning with a site analysis. You will need to prepare your soil properly, choose what method you will use to plant the lawn (seeding or sodding), then plant the lawn and care for it until it is established.

Flat areas are the best choices for lawns.

Site Analysis

Lawn installation requires that you do a site analysis and answer some simple questions before any work can begin.

- Is the area in question appropriate for a lawn? Relatively flat areas with good drainage in full sun are the most appropriate for turfgrass and are the easiest to maintain. Sloped areas, depending on the amount of the slope, are often more appropriate for other kinds of plants. Slopes exceeding a 6% grade will have an increased amount of surface runoff during irrigation or rainfall, but are still acceptable for a home lawn. Slopes greater than this will take extra work to mow, water and fertilize. Slopes greater than 15% grade are best for other plants.
- What will the lawn be used for? Will it be an entertainment space, a play area, strictly ornamental, a method of erosion control or a groundcover for ditches and unmaintained areas?
- How big does the lawn need to be for the desired usage?
- How much work is required to install the lawn?

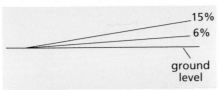

Slopes-Grade Percentages

Sloped areas present additional maintenance challenges.

Answering these questions will help guide you to make appropriate choices for your home lawn installation, such as which turfgrass species to choose, whether you will be able to install the lawn yourself, or if hiring a professional would be more appropriate.

Soil Preparation

Soil preparation is the key to establishing a good lawn, whether you are installing a new lawn or re-establishing an old one. Good soil preparation may eliminate the need for watering in areas with sufficient rainfall, such as the New England area. If you are re-establishing an old lawn, remove all the old sod and compost it before beginning. The old sod can also be repeatedly rototilled, which conserves the existing organic matter by breaking it up and incorporating it into the soil. Begin preparing the area in late spring once the soil has warmed. Ensure that the soil has good water infiltration,

good aeration and good drainage. A proper subgrade and grade will need to be established to ensure good surface and subsurface drainage. Any persistent weeds will need to be controlled, and rocks and other foreign matter may need to be removed. Any soil modification is best done at this time, including adding any fertilizers, lime or other amendments. A final surface preparation can then be made for seeding or sodding. It is a good idea to plan in advance for topography, drainage, irrigation and ornamental plantings.

Get your soil tested. This includes both the standard soil test and the food-web assay. These soil tests will let you know what amendments, if any, need to be incorporated into your soil before planting. If you tell the people at the soil-testing facilities that you are installing a lawn, they can make detailed recommendations for your soil.

Drainage

Lawn grass species need well-drained soil. You can use the drainage test

This lawn is a candidate for re-establishment.

Old, exposed tree root

described on page 39 to check how well your soil or subsoil drains. If your soil or subsoil has poor drainage, it can be corrected by adding lots of good-quality compost or compost tea. You can add a soil amendment (based on a soil test), such as gypsum. If the subsoil layer is impenetrable and unworkable, or if it is a low area that stays wet, you can install drainage tile.

Soil particle size is one influence on the drainage properties of your soil; slope is another. Rocky soil on a hillside will drain very quickly, whereas low-lying areas with fine soil particles retain water longer, and some areas may rarely drain at all.

Never add sand to clay soils. Doing so can make your soil as hard as concrete. University research shows that adding copious amounts of organic matter to clay soil is the best way to turn it into a good growing medium with better drainage. To improve compacted subsoil, or any subsoil, cultivate as deep as possible. Add 2–4" of high-quality compost and cultivate again before proceeding with placing or replacing the topsoil.

Often, new homes do not have any topsoil when the owners take possession. The layer of clay around the property will often be very compacted because of current construction methods and the use of heavy equipment. Many homes have basements, and the most common method of digging that hole is to leave the subsoil piled nearby. Eventually, the pile is leveled off once the home is built.

These construction methods severely compact the subsoil, reducing the amount of pore space in the soil, including the capillary pores. Capillary pores are important as they facilitate the upward movement of moisture between soil particles. Jack Wetmore, IPM projects coordinator for New Brunswick Horticultural Trades Association (NBHTA) and Environment Committee chair for the Canadian Nursery and Landscape Association, along with biologist and educator Ken Browne, describe the importance of capillary activity in their book *Sustainable Turf: Construction, Maintenance, and IPM Guidelines for Atlantic Canada* (2003):

Capillary action is probably the single most important factor in the underlying soil profile that determines turf growth. It is also probably the most commonly overlooked factor! It is estimated that over 95% of turfgrass moisture needs are supplied by capillary action, with moisture being drawn from as deep as 3 m [10 ft] in silt loam soils. Most natural soil profiles in this region have sufficient moisture storage capacity to ensure that lawns stay green throughout the summer. However, the capillary moisture path upward is often disrupted during construction activity, resulting in the need for irrigation to keep the lawn green. It is notable that even a 25 mm [1 in] layer of a very

Modern construction methods compact the subsoil, often severely restricting air and water movement.

different soil type can block capillary flow to the surface.

Authors Wetmore and Browne stress the importance of ensuring that the capillary pores in the soil are unobstructed so that the turfgrass is able to draw water from as deep as possible in the soil. Crushed capillary pores do not allow upward water movement. A layer of soil that is texturally different from the topsoil can also obstruct capillary action. This often occurs in new home construction when a load of topsoil is placed directly over the clay subsoil. This creates an impassible soil interface that doesn't allow water to move downward past the topsoil layer, or upward as just described. When you have a soil interface that does not allow the free flow of water downward you have a 'perched' water table. Water will not move downward until the entire soil profile above the interface is saturated, and if the subsoil is compacted clay that does not allow water to move through it, you now have a drainage problem. Soil below the perched water table is often dry.

Removing weeds

An important part of soil preparation is the control of any perennial weeds such as quack grass, creeping harebell, nutsedge and dandelions. It is a good idea to do a site assessment of the weeds, before disturbing the ground, to decide on the best way to deal with the process of weed removal. There are no methods that will get rid of all the weeds in an area, including seeds and plants. Some weeds have extensive underground root systems and take time and effort to control.

Several nontoxic methods are available for weed removal. The first is good, old-fashioned digging. Digging and physical removal gets rid of many

Drainage Test

Try this simple method of checking how quickly water drains from the soil. Dig a test hole 1 foot in diameter and 1 foot deep. Fill the hole to the top with water and let it drain completely. Fill the hole with water again and note the time. Note the time again when the water has completely drained from the hole. A drainage rate of ½" or less per hour is considered poor and may require expensive drainage work to alleviate the problem.

weeds and their associated parts. This process does not remove any seeds that are in or on the soil, though, and in the case of perennial weeds, a whole new plant can start if you miss a small portion of the roots or underground stems. Be sure to remove as much of the root system of the weeds as possible.

The next method is solarization, which involves covering the soil with a thick sheet of plastic. This kills the existing vegetation and many of the seeds in the soil seed bank. However, it also favors anaerobic soil microorganisms, which will need to be dealt with in the next phase of the soil-preparation process.

Another method for weed control is the starvation method, which depletes the carbohydrate reserve in the weeds' root systems. This method can take a whole season to be effective, but it can be accomplished in a couple of ways. One way is to remove all the top growth, till the area, wait for new top growth to appear, and then repeat the whole process. However, the increased tilling will lower the soil microorganism population. The simpler version of this method is to remove the top growth of the weeds, wait until new growth appears and then repeat the process. Removing the top growth is easily accomplished with a hoe. The young top growth can be added to your compost pile. However, do not add plants that contain seedheads to your compost pile, as the seeds may not be completely destroyed by the composting process. You can also use a flame weeder to remove the top growth. This method does not pollute the soil, but it does pollute the air. Flame weeding is most effective when the flame is passed briefly over the plant. This damages the foliage, and the plant uses up a lot of energy reserves trying to repair the damage. Frying the top growth to a crisp makes it easy for the plant to send up new leaves.

Removing rocks and other debris

Remove rocks, debris and foreign matter from as much of the rootzone as possible. Be sure to remove these items from the site—do not rebury them. Turfgrass grown above large, shallow rocks and other buried debris is subject

More of the old tree root exposed

Root that could not be removed is well below the soil surface.

These roots and 12 5-gallon buckets of weeds were removed from the site.

It is important to note that when you build the proper soil foodweb for high-quality turfgrass lawns, it makes the soil less attractive for weed species. Turfgrass is best at a 1:1 ratio of bacterial to fungal biomass. When the soil has more bacteria than fungi, it tends to favor weed growth over turfgrass.

to heat and drought stress because the root depth is limited. The same applies to old tree stumps that have been removed with a stump grinder. The stump should be ground down to a minimum depth of 8"; more is better. Any large roots should also be ground down or removed. Buried wood and stumps will eventually decay, which can lead to depressions in the turf surface. The fungal species that decompose the buried wood may also leave an unacceptable number of mushrooms on the surface. Rocks 1" in diameter and bigger can be removed. Buried debris can damage core-aerating machines.

Compost delivered to site

Subgrade

The subgrade is the grade of subsoil beneath the topsoil. If there is topsoil on the site, dig down a couple of feet to expose the subsoil layer to see if it is compacted or if there are any layers of soil that might interfere with water and air movement in the soil. If the subsoil is compacted or drains poorly (see Drainage Test, p. 39), remove all the topsoil and stockpile it, then follow the advice provided above to improve the drainage. Removing the topsoil provides an opportunity to change the subgrade and ensure that there is adequate drainage through the subsoil layer and along its surface. Your whole yard will benefit from the extra work. It may be difficult or impossible to adjust the subgrade, especially when re-establishing an existing lawn. At minimum, ensure you provide good surface drainage. The grade of the subsoil should be worked to resemble the final grade of the topsoil. Minimally, the subgrade should have a 1% slope away from buildings for surface drainage (a 1% slope means a 1 foot

Compost spread in small piles evenly over site

Small piles somewhat levelled before rototilling

Ensure compost and other amendments are mixed deeply and thoroughly.

Topsoil is a scarce and expensive resource.

rise over a 100 foot length).

Once the subgrade has had compost added and has been graded, it is time to install any hard landscaping features, such as retaining walls, patios or sidewalks, any underground irrigation system components, and any drainage tile if needed. Installing these features at this time helps alleviate soil settling below your final established grade, especially in drainage and irrigation trench lines.

Topsoil

Lawn-type turfgrasses need a minimum of 4" of topsoil, but deeper is better. It is always best to use the soil that exists on site, rather than removing it and importing topsoil. Most soils can be amended to be able to grow turfgrass and other plants. The only reason to not reuse topsoil from a site is if there is something toxic in the soil that can't be alleviated by any other means. In the case of new home construction,

you will have to import topsoil, but this will often be the topsoil that existed on the construction site before building began. Always select stone-free, screened topsoil if importing topsoil onto the site. It is a good idea to have any topsoil tested before purchasing it. This can reduce potential soil problems before they become part of your landscape.

Topsoil has become a scarce and expensive material. We only have what is present on the planet. When you import topsoil from another site, it degrades the site where the topsoil was removed.

Once you are satisfied with the subgrade and have finished installing any features, it is time to replace or place the topsoil. Evenly spread half your stockpiled topsoil, 1–2" of compost, and half of any soil amendments recommended by a soil test and cultivate again. This helps reduce any soil texture interface problems with the subsoil. Evenly spread the remaining topsoil, amendments and another 1–2" of compost on the surface and cultivate again. Ensure all soil amendments are well incorporated into the rootzone. If you have installed drainage tile or underground irrigation, ensure you do not cultivate it along with the soil. The topsoil can be piled a little deeper alongside the tile or irrigation, the amendments mixed

Establishing a final grade

in, and then the amended soil placed around the tiles or irrigation system.

Grading

Grading is an important step in ensuring your new lawn turns out well. Generally, the surface grade should match the subgrade. You want to ensure that the final grade is smooth, with no ridges, sharp drops or sudden rises that create unmowable areas. There should be a minimum slope of 1% for surface drainage.

Rake the soil to a relatively smooth surface. Borrow or rent a landscape rake for this task. When raking, keep the handle of the rake as horizontal as is comfortable for you. Rake in multiple directions. Use the flip side of the rake head to identify and correct humps and hollows. After raking, roll the soil with a water-filled lawn roller, which you can also rent.

Water the area with a sprinkler or your irrigation system. Now is the time to adjust the heads on your irrigation system to ensure good coverage. Let the soil get wet enough that there is some standing water. This will expose any remaining humps and hollows. Allow the soil to dry, then rake it and roll it again.

Allow the soil to settle before seeding or sodding. It is a good idea to complete your soil preparation by late summer or early fall, and then allow it to settle over the winter. The soil can also be settled with a few deep waterings, or with a water-filled lawn roller. The soil will need to be graded again after settling. You should be able to walk flat-footed on the prepped seed bed in flat-soled shoes and not leave footprints more than ¼" deep.

A landscape rake works better when the handle is more horizontal than vertical.

Final grade established and ready for seed.

Bentgrass lawn

Choosing a Planting Method

Most lawns are grown from seed or transplanted as sod. These two methods are, by far, the easiest for planting a lawn. Other methods include planting plugs, sprigs and stolons. No matter what method you choose, if your soil is adequately prepared, your chances for a beautiful lawn rise dramatically. There are pros and cons to consider when choosing seeding or sodding. With seeding, you get to select the turfgrass species you desire; with sod you get what the sod producer has chosen, unless you order custom-grown sod. It takes longer for a lawn to mature when grown from seed. Sod, which is a collection of mature grass plants being transplanted, creates a usable lawn much quicker. The existing soil and the soil layer on the sod may be incompatible, and may create an interface layer where infiltration of water and air is restricted. One good thing is that the soil preparation for both seed and sod is relatively the same. The process of laying sod takes longer and is more physically demanding than spreading seeds, but there are fewer weeds to deal with when sodding as compared to seeding, and sodding is better for erosion control than seeding as it provides instant, mature cover.

Seeding

Seeding is the easiest and least expensive method of planting a lawn. As seeding provides you with the flexibility to grow the exact type of lawn you desire, it is important to select the appropriate seed mix or blend for your purpose. You would not want to grow low-maintenance, reclamation grasses for a lawn where the kids play and where you host garden parties or barbecues. Conversely, you would not plant a blend of Kentucky bluegrass cultivars in a low-maintenance ditch. For the best results, start with good-quality seed. You will have to determine how much seed you will need, when you will do the seeding and what method you will use. Finally, proper post-seeding care and maintenance will ensure a quality finished product.

Turfgrass seed loses viability over time. If the seed you are using is more than a year old, you should increase your seeding rate to make up for the reduced percentage of germinating seeds.

Seeds

Use good-quality seed. Seed lots are tested for purity and germination rate. Seed purity is a measure of the percentage of turfgrass seed, other grass seeds, weed seeds and inert material in the lot. The germination rate is the percentage of seed in the lot that germinates.

Quality turfgrass seed is available across the United States. Look for Certified seed where possible. Certified seed is a quality designation specified in the Federal Seed Act. The germination rate is also noted by percentage. Certified seed has a high rate of germination, and is mostly free of weed seeds, other grass species and other debris. Certified seed is also an assurance that the variety listed on the label is the one the turfgrass breeder actually developed. Certified seed in the United States will have a blue tag on the package or bag. Be aware that the pre-packaged, mixed lawn seed that is available in large chain stores might not have the best choice of grass species for your area. Also note that there are weed seeds and other seeds that already exist in the soil (the soil seed bank), that often cause more problems than weed seeds in a seed mix.

Choosing the right turfgrass for your lawn

The United States, geographically and climatically speaking, is quite diverse, and no one blend or mixture of turfgrass will work for all locations. In the northern US, many home lawns are a mixture of Kentucky bluegrass and various fescue species such as creeping red fescue and Chewings fescue, or Kentucky bluegrass mixed with perennial ryegrass. For coastal areas of the Pacific Northwest, home lawns are most often a mixture of ryegrass and fescue, but bentgrass lawns are also grown. Tall fescue, zoysiagrass and Bermuda grass are used for lawns in the transition zone. See the turfgrass plant descriptions for more information on the environmental conditions and specific maintenance requirements for best performance of each species.

Kentucky bluegrass lawn

Seeding rate

The seeding rate is the amount of seed you will apply over a given area, and is usually measured as pounds of seed per 1000 ft² (see chart). The seeding rate depends on the type of grass used and the way the grass grows. Bunch-type grass, such as fescue, will need a slightly higher seeding rate than grass that spreads by rhizomes or stolons. Grass seed differs in size from species to species. Generally, 15–25 seeds per in² is a good rate for new lawns, depending on the turfgrass species chosen (see chart). Lower seeding rates can be used, but with the open areas of soil there is a risk of weed invasion and soil heating. Higher seeding rates are not good because individual plants will be spindly and weak, with few leaves per plant, and plants will be susceptible to stress and attacks from pests and disease. The initial growth is dense, but there is crowding and competition for water and nutrients. The stronger plants will eventually dominate the lawn, but it may take a couple of seasons.

Even seed distribution is important.

Approximate Number of Seeds Per Pound and Normal Seeding Rates
Adapted from Table 16-2 from *Turfgrass: Science and Culture* by James B. Beard

Turfgrass species	Approximate # of seed per pound	Normal seeding rates	
		lb/1000 sq. ft.	seeds/sq. in.
Bentgrass: colonial	8,723,000	0.5-1.0	30-60
Bentgrass: creeping	7,890,000	0.5-1.0	27-55
Bentgrass: velvet	11,800,000	0.5-1.0	41-81
Bluegrass: Kentucky	2,177,000	1-1.5	15-23
Fescue: Chewings	546,000	3.5-4.5	13-17
Fescue: creeping red	546,000	3.5-4.5	13-17
Fescue: tall	227,000	6-9	11-14
Ryegrass: perennial	227,000	7-9	11-14
Other grass species (includes warm season turfgrasses)	Approximate # of seed per pound	Normal seeding rates	
		lb/1000 sq. ft.	seeds/sq. in.
Bermuda Grass (hulled)	1,787,000	1-1.5	12-19
Blue Grama Grass	898,000	1.5-2.5	9-16
Bluegrass: Canada	2,495,000	1-1.5	17-26
Bluegrass: rough	2,540,000	1-1.5	18-26
Buffalograss	50,000	3-6	1-2
Fescue: hard	575,000	3.5-4.5	13-17
Fescue: sheep	530,000	3.5-4.5	13-16
Redtop	4,990,000	0.5-1.0	17-34
Fairway wheatgrass	324,000	3-5	7-11
Zoysiagrass	1,369,000	2-3	19-28

Amount of seed required

Ensure you have the proper amount of seed for the size of your lawn. Here is how to calculate how much of each type of seed is required for a mixture or blend. Divide the area of your lawn by 1000, when the lawn is measured in square feet. Multiply this number by the seeding rate and the percentage of each different seed in the mixture or blend (lawn area/1000 x seeding rate x % seed type in mixture or blend).

Using a blend of cultivars within a specific turfgrass species increases the diversity of your lawn. For example, if your lawn seed mixture requires a 60% Kentucky bluegrass component, you could easily use five different cultivars with three at 10% each and the other two at 15% each. The low end of the seeding rate is enough to grow a healthy lawn and will be used for these calculations.

For a home lawn 1500 square feet in size, composed of a mixture of 65% Kentucky bluegrass, 20% creeping red fescue and 15% perennial ryegrass, and seeded at the low rate, you will need approximately 1 pound of Kentucky bluegrass, 1 pound of creeping red fescue and 1½ pounds of perennial ryegrass.

- Kentucky bluegrass: 1500/1000 x 1 x 65% = 0.975 lbs (round up to 1 lb)
- Creeping red fescue: 1500/1000 x 3.5 x 20% = 1.05 lbs (round down to 1 lb)
- Perennial Ryegrass: 1500/1000 x 7 x 15% = 1.58 lbs (round down to 1½ lbs)

Here are some examples of home lawn mixtures for some different situations.

Zone 2 to 8:

Sunny, high-maintenance lawn
- 100% bentgrass
(Note: 5% annual or perennial ryegrass can be added to the following Zone 2 to 8 mixtures as a nurse crop)

Sunny, medium-maintenance lawn
- 60% Kentucky bluegrass
- 40% fine fescues

Sunny, lower-maintenance lawn
- 65% fine fescue
- 35% Kentucky bluegrass

Shaded areas
- 100% fine fescue

Zone 5 to 8 (+ all of the above):

Sunny, medium-maintenance lawn
- 65% Kentucky bluegrass
- 20% fine fescue
- 15% perennial ryegrass

Sunny, low- to medium-maintenance lawn #1
- 75% tall fescue
- 25% Kentucky bluegrass

Sunny, low- to medium-maintenance lawn #2
- 100% tall fescue

Sunny, low-maintenance lawn
- 65% fine fescue
- 20% Kentucky bluegrass
- 15% perennial ryegrass

Shaded areas
- 100% fine fescue

Transition Zone (including zone 5-8 mixtures):

Sunny, medium-maintenance lawn
- 100% Zoysiagrass

Sunny, medium- to high-maintenance lawn
- 100% Bermuda grass (south transition zone only)

Best time to seed

The timing of the seeding process can enhance or be a detriment to good establishment of your new lawn. The best time to seed is just prior to the onset of optimum moisture and temperature for good seed germination, but seeding can take place whenever soil moisture and temperature are favorable for seed germination. The young seedlings have the best survival rate when seeded in late summer. They will be better able to handle adverse weather, such as drought, the following growing season. Early spring is the next best time. It is important to note that when seeding in early spring to mid-summer, there will be more competition from broadleaf annual weeds (you got rid of all the perennial weeds before you seeded) than when seeding in late summer. Mid-summer seeding should only be done if the seedbed can be kept moist, weed free and relatively cool. Excessive soil temperatures that may occur during hot weather can fry the little seedlings. You want to avoid seeding in late fall when there is still an opportunity for the seeds to germinate and begin growing. The tiny seedlings are subject to frost heave in the spring, and their tiny root systems may not hold them in place.

Dormant seeding is seeding late in the fall when environmental conditions do not favor seed germination. Often used in places where the soil is too wet to work in the spring, dormant seeding works best in areas where there is good, continuous snow cover. Dormant seeding does not work very well in areas that are subject to soil erosion.

Seeding methods

Be sure to distribute the seed evenly over the lawn area, whether for a new

You can opt for pre-germinated seed. Pre-germinated seed establishes rapidly, especially when the temperature is on the cool side. This seed must be planted into moist soil immediately after germination. Sowing pre-germinated seed into dry soil desiccates the seeds rapidly. Ensure the soil remains moist after planting.

lawn or for overseeding. For smaller lawns, you can use a mechanical spreader, such as a drop spreader or a rotary spreader, or you can sow the seed by hand. Hand sowing is also known as the 'feeding the chickens' method, and can lack the uniform distribution possible with a mechanical spreader. Drop spreaders provide the most uniform seed distribution. Rotary, or cyclone, spreaders can cover an area faster than a drop spreader. Rotary spreaders tend to throw heavier seed farther than lighter seed, so distribution of a seed mixture with different sized seeds may be uneven. If using a rotary spreader with two different sizes of seed, apply one type of seed first, then adjust the spreader and apply the

Drop spreaders are easy to use and more accurate than rotary spreaders.

second type of seed. This principle can be applied to drop seeders as well, if the seed sizes or seeding rates are different. It just means you will make more passes with your spreader.

Before beginning the seeding operation, calibrate your spreader: simply adjust it so it releases the proper amount of seed for the speed you will be pushing it. As stated above, you want an average of 15–25 seeds per square inch. Get a piece of cardboard and cut out a 1" square. On a sidewalk or driveway, make a short pass with your spreader at the speed you will be using it on the lawn. If you are not sure how fast the seed will come out of the spreader, set the spreader openings for a minimal flow to begin. Randomly place your cardboard cutout in a few places where you spread the seed and count how many seeds are in the opening of the cutout. This count will be half of the full rate (see below), so you should be counting 7–12 seeds for each square-inch sample.

Before seeding new lawns, give the whole area a good soaking to moisten the soil to a depth of at least 6", if not more. Do this the day before you plan to seed, as this will allow the soil to drain of excess water. On the day you plan to seed, lightly rake the soil surface. This provides some grooves for the seeds to sit in and makes it easy for you to see your spreader tracks so it is easier to maintain the proper spreader spacing for each pass. It is also an opportunity to adjust the final grade if any unwanted humps or dips appear. For good seed coverage, divide the total amount of seed in half and apply in two different directions perpendicular to each other. Always ensure seed mixtures and blends are well mixed. After spreading the seeds, give the whole area

Rotary spreaders deposit more seed (or fertilizer) in the center of the pass than to the outside of the pass. To take a proper calibration sample, you need to make two passes. The proper spacing between passes occurs when the farthest flung seeds (or fertilizer) of the second pass just reach the middle of the first pass. Take your sample from the area in between the passes.

Typical home rotary spreader

another light rake to help cover the seeds with soil. Roll the area with a water-filled roller to ensure good seed-to-soil contact, then lightly water the area to moisten the soil surface.

Your goal is to incorporate the seed into the top layer of the soil, no deeper than $2/5$". Seeds sown on the soil surface need constant moisture and are subject to movement by wind and water. Roll the freshly seeded soil for good seed to soil contact. Rollers with ridges help with erosion control. Some larger seeders have built-in ridges on the rollers that form pockets that trap moisture

A water-filled roller ensures good seed-to-soil contact.

Young plants starting to grow

Post-seeding care

Post-seeding care is critical if you want a healthy lawn. Proper care includes watering, weeding, mowing and protecting the new seedlings.

Watering during this establishment period is critical for germination of the seeds, and the health and survival of the seedlings. The soil must remain moist (not soggy) for the first three weeks to a month. Allowing the soil to dry out is the biggest cause of seeding failure. Begin with frequent, light watering on a daily basis. This may mean a light watering a couple of times a day, or more if the weather is hot and sunny. As the plants mature, you can water deeper and less often. Eventually, you will be watering deeply about once a week, or when necessary.

Applying mulch, especially in erosion-prone areas and in areas with hot and drying winds, helps keep the soil moist. Use a loose, 2–3" layer of straw mulch to aid in establishment. Too much mulch will block sunlight and air movement, which can provide a good environment for disease to develop. You can gently remove the mulch after about one month, or sooner depending on how quickly your turfgrass is growing, or you can leave the mulch, which will break down and add organic matter to the soil.

Pull any weeds by hand when they are large enough to easily see and grab. Do not wait too long, as some weeds

and heat, aiding seed germination and plant development. Always seed when there is very little to no wind as some seeds are very light and may be blown to areas when grass is not desired.

Hand sowing can be used for seeding smaller areas. Use string and stakes to make a grid, with the grid squares being 1 square yard in size. Divide the total weight of your seed mix by the number of squares in your grid. Weigh out the appropriate amount for each square and evenly distribute the seed into the square by hand. If you have done your calculations correctly and have done a fairly good job of distribution, you should have the same number of seeds per square inch as with a mechanical spreader.

If you are seeding on a slope, you must provide some form of erosion control. You can cover the slope with jute or cellulose matting after seeding is complete or you can use a hydroseeding service. Hydroseeding applies a slurry of seed, fertilizer and mulch over an area in a single operation. Hydroseeding is good for slopes and areas where other seeding methods are impractical, and for soils with good moisture levels. One drawback is that the seed is not always in good, solid contact with the soil.

Germination occurs when the seed takes in water and begins growth. Emergence is when the germinated seed establishes roots and pushes the top growth above the soil surface. Establishment is the successful growth of the seedlings into the beautiful lawn you envisioned.

can develop deep or extensive root systems quickly. DO NOT use any pesticides, especially herbicides (organic lawn, remember!) as they can damage the young plants.

Do your first mowing when the grass reaches 3–4" in height. For the first two to three times, cut the grass to 3" in height. The cutting height can then be lowered to 2½". The first mowing will help the grass to thicken up and will take care of any annual weeds that have grown along with the new grass seedlings. Mow as you would your established turf. Do not allow the new grass to grow longer than one-third past your mowing height. It may seem like a good idea, as letting the grass grow higher would develop a deeper root system, but the drastic reduction in height when you mow the new grass is a severe stress on the new plants that can cause an unnecessary setback to establishing the lawn.

No fertilizing should be necessary for a year or more if soil preparation was adequate.

Keep as much traffic off the young seedlings as possible, as they are vulnerable to mechanical damage. You will be at the mercy of insects until the lawn is established. The development

After first mowing

Lawn was seeded right to tree base, as this tree is slated for removal.

After third mowing

Implementing insect control on newly seeded turfgrass can cause unnecessary stress on the turfgrass. That said, there will not be a large number of insects that will attack your newly seeded lawn, as most insect pests (especially the root feeders) prefer mature stands of turfgrass to infest.

A newly re-established, natural lawn

of disease can be minimized by proper watering, and by ensuring good air circulation over the area. Animals can be physically barred from access, or can be scared away with devices such as the Scarecrow™ (manufactured by Contech).

Reasons seeding can fail

Seeding can fail for a number of reasons. The soil surface can become crusted, thus starving the seedlings of air and water. Seeds planted deeper than ⅖" may fail to germinate. Deeply planted seeds that do germinate use up much, if not all, of their energy just

A garden weasel is effective for breaking up surface crust. The thin areas will need overseeding.

trying to get to the soil surface, resulting in a weak plant that is susceptible to environmental stresses. The seeds might have been old and lacking viability. A germination test will let you know how much viability your seeds have. The seeds may also be of poor quality or may have been damaged during harvest, transport or handling. The seedlings may have suffered from improper applications of fertilizer or pesticide. The soil may be unsuitable for seedling growth, as is true of saline soils and soils that lack the proper soil foodweb for turfgrass. The seeds or seedlings may have experienced attacks by insects, disease and animals. You can avoid these problems by following the methods outlined in this book.

Crusting can be alleviated with a number of methods. Daily irrigation helps break up crusting by the impact of the water droplets on the surface. You can also use mechanical surface disruption, such as a very light working with a garden weasel. Use caution with any method of surface disruption— you want to break up the crusting without disturbing the germinating seeds. Do not use mechanical surface disruption once the seedlings have emerged. Mulch helps keep the soil surface moist and less likely to crust. Also, be aware that some soils have a higher crusting potential, such as soils

Germination Test

Place a counted number of seeds between two moist paper towels, set them on a plate or pan, and put them in a warm, dark location. Use at least 25 seeds and ensure the seeds are spread out, but using more seeds will give you a more accurate result. Keep the paper towels moist but not wet. Check the seeds after 14 and 21 days, depending on the type of seeds. Count the number of seeds that germinate and those that do not. Calculate a percentage based on that count. If you use 25 seeds, and 15 of them germinate, your seed has an approximate viability of 60%.

Turfgrasses Germination Time (days)

Kentucky Bluegrass	*14–21*
Creeping Red Fescue	*7–14*
Chewings Fescue	*7–14*
Tall Fescue	*7–14*
Perennial Ryegrass	*3–7*
Creeping Bentgrass	*7–14*
Colonial Bentgrass	*7–14*
Velvet Bentgrass	*7–14*
Zoysiagrass	*10–14*
Bermuda Grass	*7–15*

English daisy in lawn

high in organic matter and soils with a high clay or silt content.

'Eco-Lawns'

An 'eco-lawn' is a mixture of grasses, flowers and herbs that stands up well to mowing. Eco-lawns are being developed by Professor Tom Cook at Oregon State University in Corvallis, Oregon. Professor Cook notes that an eco-lawn isn't an unkempt meadow; eco-lawns can be used like any conventional lawn. He and other researchers have studied various combinations of grasses and broadleaf plants to see what thrives under a mowing regime. The goal of the research is to develop ecologically stable, persistent mixtures that require fewer inputs than conventional lawns.

Some of the plants used in the Oregon trials include perennial ryegrass, Kentucky bluegrass, yarrow (*Achillea millefolium*), Roman chamomile (*Anthemis nobilis, Chamaemilum nobile*), English lawn daisy (*Bellis perennis*) and clover (*Trifolium repens*). The test plots received little to no fertilizer, were watered once a month (about 1½" of water per application), and clippings were returned to the soil. There were no significant weed problems reported.

It is my belief that these new eco-lawns closely resemble the lawns that were grown before the advent of chemical herbicides. At minimum, try to use some clover in your seed mix, but no more than ¼ lb per 1000 ft². Dutch white clover is the most appropriate clover for lawns. Finer-leafed selections of white clover that are commonly used in Europe are being investigated for use in North America.

Sodding

Sodding provides an instant lawn, but it is more expensive than seeding, especially for large areas. Sodding is basically the transplanting of mature turfgrass plants. Strips of sod are cut from large fields and stacked on pallets as rolls or slabs. This type of sod is most available for home installations.

Use good-quality sod—quality is more important than price when purchasing sod. Good-quality sod is often grown from seed. Some sod is

Dutch white clover in lawn

regenerated from the rhizomes of previously harvested sod and may not be as good a quality as seed-grown sod if the original sod contained some non-rhizomatous turfgrass. Good sod will be grown from the best available turfgrass cultivars. Always ask sod suppliers about how they grow their sod and what grass species and cultivars they are using. They are usually more than willing to supply that information as well as the names and addresses of people or companies that have recently installed a new lawn. Local growers will also make sure the sod they grow is appropriate for the local climate conditions. Locally grown sod has a better chance of having the same soil as your home area.

Good sod will have a uniform depth. All the sod pieces will be similar in thickness when they are cut from the field. Thickness refers to the thickness of the soil. A good thickness for Kentucky bluegrass-fescue sod is ¾", for ryegrass 1", and for bentgrass ½" or less. Zoysiagrass and bermuda grass sods are cut at ½–¾" thickness. The growth should be dense and the roots should be knit together well enough for easy handling. Poorly knit sod falls apart easily. The sod should be free of weeds, insects and disease, and the color should be uniform. There should be lots of roots for quick recovery from the stress of being transplanted, and there should be minimal thatch.

If you plan to use sod, it is a good idea to check the sod before you buy it to see if the soil it was grown on closely resembles the soil you have. If the soils are too different texturally (e.g., a sandy loam vs. a clay loam) there can be an interface problem and the sod roots will not grow into the on-site soil. Using sod with soil that closely matches your home soil definitely improves the chances for a successful sod installation.

Prepare the area where you will be installing the sod (see p. 36). The area should be ready to go before the sod arrives on the site. You want to lay the sod as soon as possible; sod in a stack acts as a compost pile and begins heating from the center of the stack outward, cooking the sod. The more lush and moist the sod, the faster the stack will heat up. A temperature of 105° F will kill Kentucky bluegrass, and temperatures in the center of a sod stack can easily climb much higher than that. Sod with long grass will heat quicker than sod with short grass. Sod harvested when the air or soil temperature is hot will heat up quicker in a sod stack. If you are unable to lay all the sod in one day, store it in a cool, dry place. Lay the pieces of sod out if they are not going to be used soon, and keep them moist.

Rolled sod is easy to install.

There is a good chance that the sod you buy was not grown organically. However, many sod farms are using IPM (see p. 102) as part of their management plans, which is a big step toward going totally organic. The higher the consumer demand for organic sod, the more the sod growers will provide it. We have to be the ones to ask for this kind of product if we expect the industry to produce it.

Use boards to minimize soil and sod disturbance while cutting in patches.

Sod is cheaper if you pick it up from a sod depot rather than have it delivered. You should be aware, however, that sod weighs an average of 2–6 pounds per ft^2, depending on thickness and moisture content. The average pallet holds around 360 square feet of sod. Therefore, one pallet of sod can weigh, roughly, from 800 to 2200 pounds. You should be sure your vehicle can handle the weight, as it will tend not to steer well when the front wheels are dangling in the air.

Rapid rooting is critical to the success of your sod installation. Proper soil preparation, adequate soil moisture and good laying techniques will help ensure quick rooting. Laying sod on dry soil will delay rooting, even when the area is soaked after laying it in place. Sod can be laid at any time of year as long as you have access to a water source. The sod needs enough time for to root before winter arrives. You can do dormant sodding, but only in areas where snow cover is assured.

The day before you plan to sod, soak the whole area to a minimum 6" depth. On the day you are sodding, ensure the surface of the soil is moist, but not soaked.

Begin laying the sod pieces along a straight edge, such as a driveway, sidewalk or building. Avoid starting on a curve. You can avoid soil and sod disturbance by walking on boards or planks as you work, especially in areas that may be a little soft owing to climate and time restrictions.

Ensure the pieces of sod form tight seams. The edges of the sod pieces should be snug up against each other but not overlapping. Any gaps will quickly dry out. Do not stretch the sod pieces to fit. Stretched sod will contract faster than unstretched sod as it dries, creating unnecessary gaps.

To ensure tight seams, use a carpet or linoleum knife to trim edges, cut in patches and remove overlapped pieces. For the tightest seams, overlap the sod pieces and cut through both layers, then remove the excess. When trimming, the sod pieces should fit snuggly together like a jigsaw puzzle.

Roll the area with a water-filled roller to ensure good sod-to-soil contact. Be careful to not move any sod pieces when rolling.

Water immediately to soak the whole area. Remember that the root system is

Make sure your vehicle can handle the weight of the sod.

Cutting through two overlapping sod pieces

Removing excess sod

Remaining sod pieces fit together with tight seams.

very small (most roots were removed during harvest) and is subject to drying out. Keep the sod constantly moist (not soggy) until it has re-established its roots. Then you can begin to slowly shift your watering regime to less frequent and deeper applications. If the area you are sodding is large, you may need to water the installed sod before the whole job is done, especially if the weather is hot and dry. Thin sod needs to be watered more regularly than thicker sod.

If sodding on a slope, start at the bottom. Use landscape staples or corn dog sticks to help keep the sod pieces in position. Use at least two staples or sticks per piece of sod. The staples or sticks can be removed as the sod roots into the soil. Wooden sticks can also be gently hammered deeper into the soil. Install the rows horizontally across the slope, making sure the joints are staggered. This eliminates long, vertical seams that are subject to erosion and washout.

Mow as soon as necessary. Follow the mowing guidelines noted in this book.

There is no need to fertilize for at least a year. The sod is often grown in fertile conditions, and your properly prepared soil has all the fertility your sod requires.

Annual weeds can be pulled once the sod has rooted into the soil. There will be much less weeding when sodding than when seeding, especially if you have taken care of any perennial weeds during your soil preparation.

It is best to allow as little traffic as possible on the newly sodded area until the sod has firmly rooted. Sodded lawns can be used much sooner than seeded lawns.

Plugging

Plugging is the use of small pieces of sod to repair damaged areas. It is similar to using a cookie cutter to remove the damaged area and replace it with a piece of sod the exact same dimensions. Special tools for plugging are available through professional

Freshly sodded lawn

turfgrass maintenance supply companies. You can use plugging to install a
lawn, but the process is slow, and is
limited to those grasses with rhizomes or stolons. Some zoysiagrass
and Bermuda grass varieties are
planted by plugging. Rolls or slabs of
sod can be cut into smaller pieces for
plugging. Sod can also be further torn
apart to create sprigs.

Sprigging

Sprigging is the planting of pieces of
rhizomes or stolons (called sprigs) in
furrows or random small holes. Sprigs
should have at least two nodes per piece.
Some species and cultivars of bentgrass
are planted in this way.

Plant sprigs in narrow rows or broad-
cast them over the soil surface. The soil
should be moist so the tiny sprigs do
not dry out. Try to keep one node above
the surface of the soil. Roll the area with
a water-filled roller to ensure good
sprig-to-soil contact. Keep the area
watered as you would for seeding.

Planting Trees and Shrubs

The best time to install trees and
shrubs is after you have completed
your soil preparation, but before you
seed or sod. The digging is easy at this
time and there is no sod to remove.
The next best planting opportunity
will be in fall of the next year, after the
turfgrass has had a chance to become
established.

Do not plant turfgrass right up to
the base of any tree or shrub. Trees and
shrubs have very different maintenance
requirements than turfgrass. Trees and
shrubs also require a different soil
foodweb than turfgrass. It is a good
practice to have a mulched area at least
out to the dripline of the tree or shrub.
This reduces the chance of mechanical

damage, such as mower injury, to the
tree or shrub, and helps separate the
different maintenance regimes. Trees
and shrubs will also grow quicker, as
they are not competing with the turfgrass for resources.

Ensure the mulched area under the trees and
shrubs extends out to the dripline.

Base of tree has been damaged by a mower
or line trimmer.

Turfgrass Maintenance

ALL LAWN MAINTENANCE IS GOING TO COST YOU MONEY. AN ORGANIC maintenance program may seem like it is costing a lot, what with the extra testing and the more expensive fertilizer. But over time, an organic turfgrass maintenance program will save you money. As you put into practice the advice presented in this book, your fertilizer and water costs will go down because the soil under your lawn will increase its biological diversity and population.

Some of the current methods of lawn maintenance create a lot of waste. Lawn clippings are often bagged for hauling to the local landfill, and then there are the combined problems of unused or leftover pesticides and the need to dispose of the empty, still-toxic containers.

The level of maintenance practices you perform depends on the type of grass you are growing and the intended use of the area. Low-maintenance areas that see minimal usage include roadside medians and ditches, airfields, golf course roughs and hard-to-mow slopes. High-maintenance turfgrass areas are the realm of golf courses, cricket pitches, tennis courts, lawn bowling courts and sports fields. Medium-maintenance lawns are best suited for homes, businesses, industries, institutions, parks and cemeteries.

We live in a very large and diverse country, especially when it comes to the diversity of soil types, climates and turfgrass species adaptability. This section will focus on the basic cultural practices for growing a healthy, organic lawn. These practices will have to be adapted to your specific area and conditions.

Turfgrass maintenance includes mowing, edging, watering, aerating, thatch control, turfgrass nutrition and integrated pest management (IPM). You will need access to a selection of tools to make your maintenance tasks easier.

Mowing

Mowing is, by far, the most time-consuming task when maintaining a lawn, yet it is mowing that can make the difference between a healthy green carpet or a stressed-out lawn that is susceptible to pest attacks and climate changes. Mowing height is an important decision that affects the health of the grass and the depth of the roots. All grasses have a preferred range of cutting heights, and will have the deepest roots when mowed at the high end of the range. Mowing frequency is how often you mow the lawn. The more often a lawn is mowed, the thicker it becomes. The type of lawn mower you choose affects both the quality of cut and the environment (see Mowers, p. 76). We've also included some mowing tips that will help ensure a high-quality job.

Mowing height

We have all watched professional golf events on television and perhaps we've played at some well-maintained golf courses. We see the short, dense grass and we want that for our home lawns, but it may not always be possible. You

first need to know if your lawn is a species of grasses that can be cut that short. Golf courses use bentgrass, which can be cut very short. Some cultivars of Kentucky bluegrass can be cut short, but if they are cut short, they are often invaded by annual bluegrass, a prolifically self-seeding annual grass that thrives at very short heights of cut. Bentgrass is also subject to invasion by annual bluegrass. As mentioned above, all grasses have a limited, preferred cutting height range. Mowing your grass shorter than the low range for the grass causes weak, non-vigorous growth and disrupts the balance of the grass's physiological systems. The shorter the grass, the shallower the root system, and the more the turf is subject to environmental stresses.

The rule of thumb for mowing turfgrass is never cut off more than ⅓ of the leaf blade at a time. Scalping may occur when you mow the grass shorter than the desired range. Scalping happens when you remove all the green parts of the plant, leaving only the brown stems. Those of us who have used a rotary mower are familiar with scalping. Remember when your lawnmower wheel slipped off the turf edge or dropped into a depression and

It is better to allow lawn clippings to remain on the lawn, but sometimes they need to be collected.

environmental conditions, the desired cutting height and the purpose the grass is serving. Cutting the lawn activates shoot growth and tillering. Tillering is secondary, lateral shoot growth that is stimulated by removing the top portion of the turfgrass blades (mowing your lawn). Grass favors shoot growth over root growth for the available carbohydrates (see Mowing height, p. 59). When grass is cut, the plant sends its energies to shoot growth and not to root growth. The more shoots that are removed, the longer it will take for the root system to begin growing again. In optimal environmental conditions of adequate water, sunlight and temperature, and good fertility levels, vertical shoot growth will increase, which will increase the mowing frequency.

carved a closely cropped circle into the lawn? That's scalping. Places to watch for scalping when mowing are at the tops of hills and mounds and along the edge of the lawn, especially where the soil surface is higher than the adjacent surface.

Scalping may also occur when you have left the task of mowing for too long. In this case, cutting to your desired height in one fell swoop is not the best thing. If you have left your lawn for too long, then bring the height down slowly. Scalped grass uses the carbohydrate reserve in the roots for growth, depleting those reserves and making the grass subject to environmental stresses and pest attacks. Tillering, root growth and rhizome growth stop when grass is severely scalped. Root growth only begins again when sufficient shoot growth has occurred. If your grass is already in a weakened condition and is then scalped, death of the plants may be the result. There is no cure for a scalped lawn. It just needs time to recover. Avoiding scalping is the best policy.

Mowing frequency

How often you mow your lawn depends on how fast it is growing, the

Mowing frequency usually increases as the height of cut is lowered; grass used for sports and games, for example, is usually mowed more frequently than the average home lawn.

Frequent mowing results in uniform, dense, smooth surfaces. Less frequent mowing results in coarser leaf blades and a lower number of shoots. When you mow more frequently than necessary, the result is increased shoot density and increased lushness, and decreased upward shoot growth, root growth, rhizome growth and chlorophyll content. An increase in mowing frequency slows down root growth more than shoot growth.

There are times when it is not possible to mow as frequently as needed. The weather may be prohibitive, your mower may be broken, or you might go away on holidays without making arrangements to have someone mow your lawn. The best method to reduce the height of the lawn back to your

normal mowing height and to avoid scalping the lawn is to slowly lower the mowing height of the grass. This means you first raise the height of cut to remove only ¹/₃ of the grass blades. Then mow every couple of days, lowering the height of cut each time, until you are back to your normal height of cut. You can cut your lawn down to your normal height of cut all at once, but you will cause undue stress on the turfgrass. If you do lower the height all at once, you should bag the clippings or leave them on the lawn and mow over them a couple of times.

Mowing tips

- Keep an even, steady ground speed. Mowing too quickly can cause an uneven cut.
- Do not mow grass when it is wet. Dry turf cuts easier, mowers do not plug as easily and clippings do not bunch up. Also, grass is slippery when wet, which ups the risk of slipping while mowing.
- Avoid sharp turns with riding mowers as this can bruise or tear up the grass.
- Remove debris, such as rocks, sticks, garbage and metal objects from the lawn before mowing. These items can damage and dull mower blades quickly. If using a rotary mower, these objects can be tossed a good distance and can cause injury if anyone gets hit.
- Keep your mower blades sharp, balanced and properly adjusted. Cleanly cut grass continues growing with minimal setbacks, while poorly cut, mangled turf loses vigor, grows slower and is of a lower quality.
- Wear good-quality footwear with a

Mowing can be used to remove flowers and seedheads of weeds in the lawn.

good grip so you do not slip while mowing, especially on slopes. Steel-toed footwear is preferable.

- Some mowers have a bag attached to collect clippings. These clippings can be tossed on the compost pile or dried and used as mulch in the flowerbed or garden, provided the grass hasn't been treated with pesticides.
- Always clean your mowing and trimming equipment after each use. The effectiveness of mulching mowers is greatly reduced if grass clippings and debris are not removed.
- Always clean off hard surfaces, such as sidewalks and driveways, of errant grass clippings. Do not wash the clippings into the street or down sewer drains where they can cause problems. Grass clippings and fallen leaves can plug storm sewer inlets and perhaps cause flooding. Decomposing grass clippings and leaves can create an unacceptable level of nutrients, especially phosphorous, in the storm and runoff water. This can contaminate rivers, lakes and groundwater.

Mowing direction

The mowing direction is the direction and pattern you mow your lawn. Some people mow straight back and forth, some mow in circles and some mow diagonally. It is a good idea to change the mowing direction and pattern to reduce rutting caused by the mower wheels. Following the same path will eventually cause ruts to form, especially with riding mowers.

Striping

We have all seen pictures of golf courses and baseball diamonds that have fancy, striped patterns on the turfgrass. These stripes are a result of mowing with a reel mower, usually a professional quality, gas-powered reel mower. Reel mowers have a roller that is just behind the reel, and these rollers orient the grass in the direction of the mower. The stripes are visible as the sun reflects at different angles that depend on the way the grass is facing. Grass that is facing away from you will appear lighter than grass facing towards you. Striping is possible with a rotary mower, provided the mower has a roller attached to the back of it.

Edging

Edging is the process of trimming excess growth along the edges of your lawn. There are two kinds of edging for lawns. One keeps the turfgrass from growing over the edges of sidewalks, driveways and patios, and the other is the edging for flower and shrub beds adjacent to the lawn.

Edging your home lawn is not an essential maintenance task. You can choose to edge or not, but lawns with clean, trimmed edges look really good. Some species of turfgrass, especially

Freshly edged lawn

Gas-powered edger

the rhizomatous grasses such as Kentucky bluegrass, can grow quite a distance out over an adjacent concrete or other surface.

The goal of edging is to get a clean, straight line along the lawn edge, not too far in from the adjacent surface. The first method is to get an edging tool or a spade (a short shovel with a flat, square blade) and slice along the edge of the lawn, removing the overgrown bits. There is also a specially designed hand tool that looks like a wheel with teeth along one side attached to a long handle. This type of edger rolls along the solid surface, cutting a straight edge on the turfgrass as it rolls. These do a good job provided

the teeth are kept sharp. There are also gas-powered edgers that can make short work of this task. Lawn edgers are available at most places that sell garden tools.

A proper edge around a flower or shrub bed that is contained within the area of the lawn will keep turfgrass from invading the flowerbed (see diagram). If the turfgrass does invade, it is easy to

Turf edging blade
(Gardena® Combimax System)

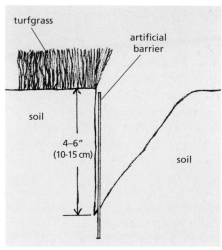

Proper bed edge

remove. This edge can be augmented with some form of physical barrier, such as the black plastic lawn edging available in most garden centers.

Watering

An important maintenance task, watering is the second most common task we do for our lawns. Proper watering helps a lawn stay healthy and able to resist damage from traffic, environmental stresses such as drought and pest problems such as disease. Poor watering practices, whether overwatering or underwatering, can seriously harm your turfgrass. You can water your lawn with a hose and sprinkler, a soaker hose or an underground irrigation system. There are also ways to reduce the water needs of your lawn.

In recent times, the use of water for lawns has become a concern for many people. The cost of water is on the rise, and in some locations there are water restrictions owing to drought conditions. There is the problem of urban sprawl, where a city's infrastructure cannot accommodate the amount of people moving into an area. There is also the idea that lawns are inefficient users of water and that less lawn in the landscape will conserve water and save money.

Proper watering

Proper watering involves watering your lawn based on the needs of the turf-grass. Depending on the turfgrass species grown and the climate conditions, lawns need about ½-1" of water per week in the summer if you're going to keep them green. Fescue-dominated lawns will require less water than Kentucky bluegrass lawns. Lawns require less water in the spring because their root systems have not regenerated

Turfgrass plants slough off the majority of their roots in the winter and grow new roots in the spring. Fall watering can be reduced because the turfgrass is preparing for winter dormancy.

Always water deeply and slowly. Deep, infrequent watering promotes deep roots, which allow the plants to better handle drought conditions and to obtain nutrients from a deeper source. Frequent, shallow watering promotes a shallow root system, which is subject to environmental and pest stresses. Set an empty tuna can (or any straight-sided can or tin) on the lawn within reach of the sprinkler. Stop watering when the can has 1" of water in it and then dump the water from the can onto the lawn, directly under where the can was sitting. Tuna cans are often just over 1" deep, so when the can is almost full, you have applied 1" of water.

If your soil is quite dry, if your lawn puddles or if your lawn is sloped, apply ½" of water, wait a couple of hours, and then apply the other ½". This method reduces the amount of water lost through runoff and evaporation. Apply water only as quickly as the soil can absorb it.

When to water

Professional turfgrass managers base their watering on the evapotranspiration (ET) rate of the turfgrass: the total amount of water lost from turfgrass plant transpiration (giving off water as part of its physiological processes) plus evaporation of water from the soil surface. Turf managers know that the ET rate is not a constant value, but changes with the seasons and the weather. Turf managers will adjust their watering regime to reflect the

Water your lawn deeply and only when necessary, especially when there are trees and shrubs nearby.

changing ET rates. These are the same conditions we must pay attention to for watering our home lawns. If it is cool and rainy, your turfgrass will not need as much water as when the weather is hot and dry. Watering your lawn on a fixed schedule (every Tuesday and Saturday, for example) is never a good practice.

There are some easy methods to determine if the lawn needs water. The first method is the footprint test. This test involves walking across the lawn and observing your footprints in the lawn. If the turfgrass remains flattened and does not spring back within a short time, it is time to water. A second

method is to observe the color of the grass. If the grass looks vibrant and green then the grass does not need water. A dull, bluish gray color indicates a lack of water. You can also use a soil moisture meter, which is a type of probe that reads the moisture content of the soil. Turfgrasses recover quickly if watered very soon after a need is identified. If you wait too long to water, the lawn might go dormant.

A simple probe can be used to check if you have watered deeply enough to moisten the whole rootzone. A probe can be anything from a long screwdriver to a piece of coat hanger. Push the probe into the soil to a depth of 8" in heavier soil and 12" in lighter, sandy soil. If the probe pushes in easily to the suggested depth, you have watered deeply enough. If the probe is difficult to push into the soil to the suggested depth, you have not watered deeply enough. You can also use a manufactured professional soil probe, which allows you to actually see the moisture level in the soil.

Overwatering and underwatering

Overwatering reduces the vigor and quality of the turfgrass, lowers the available oxygen in the soil, reduces shoot and root growth, and promotes disease (many diseases require free water for their growth). Overwatering leaches plant-available nutrients from the rootzone, destroys soil structure, makes playing surfaces unsafe and wastes water through runoff, evaporation and overspraying (watering the concrete beside the lawn). Overwatering is also a waste of money.

Underwatering leads to thin, poorly growing, ugly-looking turfgrass of low vigor. Underwatered turf does not recover as quickly from injury or other stresses.

Tips on lowering your water usage

Apply water in the early morning. This gives the water a chance to penetrate into the soil, which reduces water loss through evaporation, and it gives the grass blades a chance to dry during the heat of the day, which reduces the possibility of disease. Fungal diseases only grow when certain environmental conditions are present, such as a certain temperature and humidity, and often moisture on the leaf surfaces for a certain length of time. Any watering that extends the length of time that the leaf surfaces remain moist will increase the risk of disease development.

Choose a turfgrass species that has lower water requirements or is better adapted to handle drought conditions. Fescue lawns are more tolerant of drought than Kentucky bluegrass.

Aerate your lawn to relieve compaction and excess thatch. Compacted soil and excessive thatch can prevent water from penetrating into the soil.

Ensure that the soil foodweb is complete and healthy. A healthy soil foodweb will help keep the soil porous, allowing water and the turfgrass roots to penetrate deeply into the soil.

Allow the turfgrass to enter **summer dormancy**. The natural growth habit of cool-season turfgrasses is to go into a period of summer dormancy. It is only because we water and fertilize that these grasses stay green in the summer (other than those summers where it is really rainy). Let your lawn go into dormancy during the heat of summer or during periods of drought. A minimum of 1" of water per dry month ($^1/_2$" every two weeks) helps keep the dormant turfgrass alive and helps it recover quicker when the weather cools in the fall. Water slowly so the water has a chance to penetrate. If you are going to be using your lawn for activities and play, it is best to keep it watered regularly. Heavy traffic on dormant lawns can cause a lot of damage to the turfgrass plants.

Watering methods

The most common method to water your lawn is with a hose and sprinkler, and there is a wide assortment of sprinklers available. You can also use soaker hoses that apply water very slowly or underground irrigation systems that come with a variety of sprinkler types.

Sprinklers

The wide variety of sprinklers on the market range from the common oscillating sprinkler to some very ornate, decorative sprinklers, to sprinklers designed with playing children in mind. Home sprinklers are made of plastic and/or metal. It is a good idea to invest in a high-quality sprinkler, but be sure that whatever sprinkler you choose does the job you need it to do.

All sprinklers will apply more water closer to the sprinkler than farther out. To water your whole lawn evenly, hose-end sprinklers will need to be moved. Watering is most efficient when the sprinklers are moved so the watering patterns overlap. This means moving the sprinkler so that the water coming sprinklers have a way to block some of the holes to narrow the width of the fan. Oscillating sprinklers apply water gently, but are affected by wind. The distribution pattern is rectangular with rounded ends. Oscillating sprinklers tend to apply more water in the center of the fan than the outer edges of the fan. Oscillating sprinklers are good for small to medium-sized lawns. This type of sprinkler needs to be connected to the water supply with a hose, and the sprinkler will need to be physically moved to provide even watering over the entire lawn.

Impact sprinklers are the sprinklers we hear before we see. These are the sprinklers that make the chik-chik-chik-chik-ch-ch-ch-ch-ch-ch-ch-ch-

Oscillating sprinkler

from the new sprinkler position just touches the previous location of the sprinkler. Irrigation systems are designed with this principle in mind.

Large droplet size can cause soil compaction, soil crusting, loss of soil structure and erosion on slopes, especially if the droplets are travelling quickly. On the other hand, large droplets are less affected by wind than finer droplets.

The most common sprinkler is the **oscillating sprinkler**. These sprinklers put out streams of water in a fan shape, with the fan moving back and forth from one side to the other. They can be adjusted to swing fully from side to side, partially from side to side, or to one side only. New models of oscillating

Impact sprinkler with platform base

Impact sprinkler with spike base

chik-chik-chik-chik sound. They have a large stream (or streams) of water that rotates by the action of a spring-loaded or weighted hammer that is driven into the sprinkler body by the force of the stream of water. The distribution pattern is circular, and many impact sprinklers can be adjusted to water in a part circle. The stream can be adjusted from a long, narrow stream to a wide stream with fine droplets. Impact sprinklers can be attached to a hose or can be part of an in-ground irrigation system. These sprinklers also apply water gently, and the stream can be affected by the wind. When attached to a hose, the sprinkler will need to be moved to provide even watering over the entire lawn. Both oscillating and impact sprinklers are effective for lawn watering.

A third type of sprinkler is the **fixed-spray sprinkler**. This sprinkler has a set pattern and applies water over the whole pattern all at once with no sprinkler parts moving while watering.

Fixed-spray sprinkler with six different spray patterns

Fixed-spray sprinklers can be attached to a hose or they can be part of an in-ground irrigation system. Hose-end types can have a single pattern or can have a variety of patterns that can be selected by turning a turret to the desired pattern. Sprinklers that have a variety of patterns are good for using on small lawns, or for watering in odd-shaped areas. Many decorative sprinklers are fixed-spray design.

Rotary-arm sprinklers are old-fashioned sprinklers with arms that

Well-maintained, natural lawns are a joy to use.

A properly watered lawn can stay green all summer!

spin in a circle when water moves through them. Travelling rotary-arm sprinklers are also available that look like little tractors with spinning arms on top. These sprinklers are geared to move slowly along the ground, guided by the hose that the sprinkler is attached to. Travelling sprinklers are good for large lawns as they minimize the need to move the sprinklers manually. Some of the more ornate, decorative sprinklers have a similar watering action to rotary-arm sprinklers.

Gear-driven rotor sprinklers put out a stream of water that turns in a circular or semi-circular pattern, similar to impact sprinklers. The turning motion is caused by water moving through an internal geared rotor, which slowly turns the stream of water. They are quiet and efficient sprinklers and can be used anywhere that impact sprinklers can be used. They are most commonly used with in-ground irrigation systems,

but have just come on the market as hose-end sprinklers.

Sprinklers designed with kids in mind are specifically for fun. They are generally inefficient at applying water to your lawn, but are a blast for your kids. It is important to realize here that all that water and foot traffic may cause some compaction and loss of soil structure, but this is no reason to stop the kids from having fun. Your regular maintenance tasks, such as aerating and the regular addition of good-quality compost or compost tea, will help alleviate any lawn problems caused by summer fun.

Irrigation systems

Home irrigation systems are becoming quite popular. The cost of home systems has really come down, especially when you install the system yourself. If you are thinking of installing an irrigation system, or having a system installed by a professional, try to learn as much as you can before you decide. Many information resources are available. Designing an irrigation system for a landscape is an involved, detailed process, and is best left to irrigation professionals. Many companies will design a system for you and sell you the parts for you to install yourself.

Home irrigation systems, when they are properly designed, installed and maintained, last a long time and have some distinct benefits. They can save you time, water and money, and also add to the value of your home. However, in-ground irrigation systems require more maintenance than a hose with a sprinkler.

Home irrigation systems save time. You no longer have to set up a sprinkler and hose or move the sprinkler to get even watering. You don't even have to be at home to turn the system on and off.

Home irrigation systems save water. A properly adjusted irrigation system applies water where it is supposed to go—onto the turfgrass (or other landscape areas). The amount of water that does not hit the turfgrass is minimized. You are not watering the concrete driveway, for example. Irrigation systems are usually connected to a timer, which turns the system on and off. Many thousands of gallons of water can be, and often are, wasted because we forget to turn the water off to a hose-end sprinkler.

Plants benefit from irrigation systems. There are times when you cannot physically be there to water your lawn. The best example of this is when you go on vacation and the weather gets hot and dry at home. A home irrigation system automatically waters your lawn and other plants while you soak up sun on the beach. Irrigation systems can be programmed to provide the correct amount of water at the best time for the plants.

A home irrigation system adds value to your property in two ways. First, it helps you maintain your home landscape. An attractive, well-maintained landscape full of healthy plants increases a home's market value. Second, a home irrigation system adds value to your home by the very fact of it having been installed. It is like having another appliance to make life easier.

In-ground irrigation systems do require maintenance. In the northern US and wherever the ground freezes, the irrigation systems must be drained of water before the ground freezes in the fall. Water expands as it freezes, and this expansion can shatter pipes, fittings, valves and sprinkler heads. Also, sprinkler heads sometimes need adjusting to make sure they are level, aimed properly and functioning correctly. An irrigation audit by a trained irrigation professional can help you get the most efficiency from your irrigation system.

Aerating

Over time, the soil under your lawn can be compacted by foot traffic,

Large lawns and landscapes are easy to water with an in-ground irrigation system.

Ensure your lawn is actively growing before you aerate. This lawn had recently broken winter dormancy and was just beginning to actively grow.

mowing, irrigation and weather. Compacted soil does not allow air or water to enter and the health of the turfgrass suffers. You will see a decline in turfgrass vitality and there often will be standing water after a rain or after watering. Severe compaction leads to bare patches, such as those seen in front of soccer goalposts on school grounds or with footpaths across a park. A freeze/thaw cycle helps keep the lawn aerated, but it might not be enough.

It is easy to check if your soil is compacted. Poke a screwdriver into the soil; if it sinks easily you do not need aeration. If the screwdriver doesn't go in easily or at all, you definitely need aeration. If compaction is severe, consider renovating the entire lawn.

Aerating relieves compaction. It allows more air and water to get into the soil, which helps the growth of plants and beneficial soil microorganisms. Aerating reduces surface runoff and

increases water infiltration speed and water retention, which reduce irrigation needs. Deep aeration allows greater penetration of fertilizers and soil amendments, such as compost and lime, into the soil. Continued deep aeration eventually disrupts and destroys undesirable layers of different soil textures present in the rootzone, such as is often the case when sod grown on one soil type is laid on soil of a different texture. Different soil textures may also occur when a layer of silt is blown in by the wind. Deep aeration improves turf resiliency and helps stimulate thatch decomposition, especially with core aeration where soil is brought to the surface. Aerating can be done with an aerating machine or by hand with a garden fork or a step-on aerator. A garden fork will open up holes in the soil with less surface disruption than core aerating, but is practical only for small lawns.

Core aerating involves removing small cores or plugs from the lawn.

After core aerating, your lawn looks like a pack of dogs had a 'party' on it. Both manual and power aerators are available for sale or rent. Water your lawn deeply the day before core aerating. Core aerating to 3" is a good target depth. Another method, shatter tine aerating, uses solid spikes or blades that shatter the soil structure to open up passages for air and water. This method is often used on golf courses where cores on the lawn would disrupt play. Shatter tine aeration works best on slightly drier soil. Some newer aerator systems use high-pressure water to open up channels in the soil. Of all the methods, core aerating is the best for home lawns.

Aerate only when the turfgrass is actively growing (spring and fall) and has a chance to recover. Never aerate dormant turf. Late fall aeration may be bad if the aeration holes stay open all winter and the turfgrass suffers from dessication. Late fall aeration can be good in really wet winters as it can minimize crown hydration and low temperature kill. Aerate in moist, not wet, soil for the best penetration. Aerate in fall if you plan to do nothing with the cores; winter weather will help break them down. If aerating in spring, you can break up the cores by dragging a weighted chain-link fence back and forth over the lawn. The holes fill with loose soil and the turfgrass roots grow in easily and quickly. You can also remove the cores and topdress the lawn with compost. This is a great time to overseed thin areas of your lawn.

Aeration does not need to be done as a regular maintenance practice, but only when needed to help correct soil compaction or localized dry spots. How often you aerate depends on the type and amount of traffic, the species of grass, the soil texture and structure, the health of the soil foodweb, and the soil water content. Aeration is also used when doing lawn renovations and overseeding. Avoid aerating when seeds such as poplar and dandelion are in abundance to avoid accidentally planting them in your lawn.

The spiked shoes that are advertised for lawn aeration may create more of a problem than they help. The spikes physically damage the grass plants and also create a compacted layer at the depth the spikes sink into owing to the increased pressure (PSI) under the spikes. These shoes are better for walking on ice than for aerating your lawn.

Topdressing

Topdressing is the distribution of a thin layer of material over a turfgrass area. The material might be soil or compost. It is used for thatch control, smoothing and leveling of the turfgrass

Topdressing can easily be applied with a shovel.

Aerating and topdressing a large lawn can be a lot of work. Consider hiring a lawn service that provides natural maintenance.

surface, covering stolons or sprigs if planting that way, adding soil microorganisms and for winter protection. If you are topdressing to level or smooth the turfgrass surface, use thin layers and ensure the topdressing soil is the same texture as the existing soil. Spread the topdressing evenly over the lawn and gently work it into the lawn with a push broom.

Thatch Control

Thatch is a tightly intermingled layer of dead and dying organic matter in various stages of decomposition. It forms a layer just above the soil surface. It is composed of grass roots, stems, rhizomes, crowns and stolons, as well as other organic debris like tree leaves and bark. These plant parts have a high lignin content, and tend to decompose slowly. Grass clippings, on the other hand, do not cause thatch build-up—clippings are 80–85% water and decompose quickly (see Grass-cycling, p. 99). However, some grass species have more fibrous tissues and a higher lignin content than other

grasses, which results in a slower decomposition process and possibly quicker thatch accumulation than other grasses.

Thatch occurs when actively growing grass deposits more dead stuff than can be removed by the soil microorganisms. Thatch accumulation is enhanced by vigorously growing turfgrass, any practices that stimulate excessive growth, acidic soils, poorly aerated soils, soils with excess nitrogen, lawns that are infrequently mowed or mowed too low, overwatering and lawns with an unbalanced or depleted soil foodweb.

Thatch decomposition decreases when soil microorganism activity is low, and increases when soil microorganism activity is high. Moist soils with soil temperatures from 70–100° F favor soil microbial activity. Compacted, waterlogged or dry soils reduce microbial decomposition activity. Chemical fertilizers and pest-control products can also reduce microbial activity.

Lawns perform better with a layer of thatch than without. The thatch improves wear tolerance, reduces soil compaction, cushions against human activity and insulates against weather extremes. A ½" thatch layer can be beneficial, but more than that can cause problems.

When thatch becomes too thick, it leads to a rise in pest insects and turfgrass diseases, localized dry spots, chlorosis (leaf yellowing owing to loss of chlorophyll), a lawn that is more prone to scalping and reduces heat, cold and drought tolerance. Thatch is the ideal environment for many insects and diseases to make their home. Thick thatch also reduces the effectiveness of fertilizers and pest-control products, which are absorbed into the thatch and don't reach their intended targets.

A thick layer of thatch prevents water from reaching the soil underneath. Localized dry spots develop when the soil dries to the point where it is hydrophobic, actually repelling water. Thick thatch can hold the water at the soil surface like a sponge, not allowing it to infiltrate into the soil.

Thick thatch makes turf feel spongy underfoot. Lawns can be scalped when the wheels of the mower sink into the thatch layer and the actual height of cut is lower than the mower's setting.

As the thatch layer thickens, it restricts air and water movement into the soil and the turfgrass crowns, roots and rhizomes migrate up into the thatch layer, where they become vulnerable to heat, drought and cold.

There is more thatch found on fine-textured soils with poor drainage. Aerobic microorganisms, especially fungi, are responsible for thatch decomposition. Breaking up aeration cores that are left on the turfgrass surface introduces soil microorganisms into the thatch, as does topdressing with compost.

Some grasses are more thatch-prone than others. Thatch for a healthy Kentucky bluegrass-red fescue lawn can be up to ½" thick. However, Kentucky bluegrass produces more thatch than most other cool-season turfgrasses and requires regular monitoring to ensure the thatch layer does not become too thick.

A naturally maintained lawn

To check the thickness of your lawn's thatch, cut out a small chunk of turf. Thatch that is thicker than ½" will have to be controlled.

Biological thatch reduction is preferred, as it is a preventive measure more than a curative measure. Excess thatch is best removed by building up the soil foodweb, especially the fungal organisms that decompose the tougher plant parts.

Thatch management options include controlling the rate of turf growth by manipulating the amount of water and fertilizer the lawn receives, stimulating the soil microorganisms responsible for thatch decomposition, topdressing with a similar soil texture soil or quality compost, and raising the pH in acidic soils. Sometimes the soil may be neutral pH, but the thatch may be acidic (see Liming, p. 17).

If the thatch layer is too thick, you may need to use mechanical means such as vertical mowing (power raking) or aerating to remove it.

A power rake is a type of vertical mower that can be rented from most equipment-rental companies. Only use a power rake if you have a lot of excess thatch; power raking on healthy lawns can do a lot of damage. Vertical mowing should bring up more dead material than living plant material. Remove the debris immediately. It is best to do any vertical mowing when the lawn has at least 30 days of active growing available after verticutting. Late summer is a good time. In early spring before new shoot growth begins also helps clean up any debris deposited over the winter. Do not verticut during active shoot growth in spring or just before high temperatures arrive in summer because recovery can be poor and slow. Also avoid vertical mowing during weed seed dispersal times.

The thatch layer is between the white lines.

Make one or two passes, remove and compost the excess, and then overseed and topdress the lawn. You can topdress the lawn with ¼" of compost or good, healthy soil.

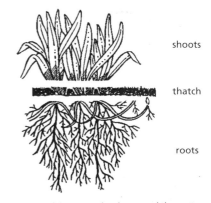

shoots

thatch

roots

Thatch occurs between the shoots and the roots

Tools and Equipment

TO MAINTAIN YOUR LAWN, YOU NEED TO HAVE ACCESS TO A SELECTION OF equipment and tools. You do not need to own all the tools, just have access to them. Some tools and equipment are covered in other sections of the book, such as seeders in the Seeding section.

Tools for Mowing

It is always best to own your own lawn mower. Your lawn mower can cut the vast majority of your lawn, but you will need some way to cut those areas that the lawn mower can't reach, such as along a fence or in a corner. This can be done with a line trimmer (string trimmer, weed eater) or a set of grass shears.

Mowers

The two main types of mowers used for lawn maintenance are reel mowers and rotary mowers. The size and topography of your lawn and the quality of cut desired will determine the type of mower needed to provide the results you want. Reel mowers and rotary mowers are both available as walk-behind units and as riding units. Riding units are good for large areas, but quite impractical for the average home lawn. Vertical mowers are used for seasonal maintenance and renovations.

There are several features to look for when choosing a lawn mower. Good quality equipment is always a good investment, and ease-of-use is an important factor. The lawn mower you use should be comfortable for you to operate. A good place to start is to check the various consumer product guides, such as Consumer Reports, for their test ratings and analysis. The mower should have a height of cut adjustment, which is important for lowering the height of your lawn when it is overgrown. Some models have one-lever height adjustment; this type of mechanism is easier to use than having to adjust each wheel individually. In those situations where it's necessary to bag the clippings, a rear-bagging mower is easier to maneuver and has a larger bag capacity than a side-bagging mower. Clipping catchers for reel mowers are always behind the reel. A good feature to have is the ability to convert from bagging to recycling/ mulching. All power mowers should have a brake engine clutch, which stops the engine when the handle is released, or a brake blade clutch, which stops the blade without stopping the engine. This last feature lets you empty the bag without having to restart the engine.

Push-type reel mower

Rechargeable electric reel mower

Reel Mowers

Reel mowers run the range from the old-fashioned push types that your grandpappy used, to high-tech, riding gas- and electric-powered units used for maintaining golf courses. Reel mowers are the best choice when dense, close-cut grass is desired. When properly maintained, they provide the highest quality of cut of any mower. They are the only type of mower able to effectively cut grass to heights lower than 1". Reel mowers perform best on smooth surfaces, and with a high frequency of cut. You need to mow more often with a reel mower than with a rotary mower, because cutting with a reel mower is ineffective when grass and other plants are taller than the horizontal centerline of the reel. This often precludes reel mowers as a choice if you are going to mow your lawn higher than 2". Generally, the higher the reel horizontal centerline, the higher you can mow your lawn.

Gas-powered convertible bagging/mulching rotary mower

engines or extension cords to worry about. They are the most environmentally friendly mowers available (other than sheep and goats) and a wonderful way to exercise. The reel doesn't throw debris, and the reel stops spinning when the mower stops moving. The old-fashioned push types are generally less expensive than rotary mowers, and there is no engine to maintain.

Rechargeable electric models are available. Walk-behind, gas-powered models are also available, but these can be prohibitively expensive for the average homeowner.

Rotary mowers

A rotary mower is the mower you most likely use to maintain your lawn. Rotary mowers are commonly used because they are able to handle a range of mowing conditions. Rotary mowers can cut tall grass and weeds, provided you are not attempting to mow a jungle. Rotary mowers are able to handle rough, bumpy lawns better than reel mowers, but tend to scalp more often than reel mowers. By changing the blade of a rotary mower, the mower can be used for cutting, recycling and vertical cutting. Rotary mowers can be used for mulching fallen leaves and for cutting back some perennials, such as goutweed and yarrow. The blades and decks of recycling mowers are designed to cause an updraft that allows clippings to be cut many times before being deposited on the lawn.

Rotary mowers can cause injury from flying debris. Make sure all the guards are in place and that the engine brake clutch is working. Keep the blade sharp and balanced. Of all the mower types listed, rotary mowers are the easiest to maintain blade sharpness.

The blades of a reel mower spin on a horizontal axis. The reel mower uses a scissors-type cutting action, with the spinning blades passing by a stationary bedknife. The more blades the reel has, the higher quality of cut it produces.

Sharpening reel mowers is an exacting process that should be done once a year by someone trained in sharpening reels. The sharpened edge can be maintained through the year by backlapping, which involves spreading an abrasive compound on the reel edges and spinning the blade backwards. Modern versions of the old-fashioned reel mower often come with, or have available, a kit for backlapping so you can do this procedure yourself.

As mentioned above, there are a few different types of reel mowers available. The typical models for homes are the old-fashioned push types. Most of these are ground-wheel driven: the reel is attached to the wheels by gears, so that when the wheels turn, the reel turns. Push-type reel mowers are very easy to use—all you do is push the mower around the lawn, with no

The blade of a rotary mower spins on a vertical axis. The cutting action of a rotary mower is a scythe-like action: the sharp blade strikes the grass and slices off the grass tips. This cutting action causes more injury to the leaf blades than does the action of a reel mower (provided both are sharp and adjusted properly). However, with a sharp blade the injury to the grass is minimal.

There are numerous types of rotary mowers available, with a choice of gas or electric models.

Electric models are the next most environmentally friendly type of mower, after push-type reel mowers. They come in corded and rechargeable types. Electric models are good for small to mid-sized lawns, and they are quiet, relatively non-polluting and easier to maintain than gas-powered types. You can cut your lawn at 6:00 in the morning without disturbing your neighbors. Electric mowers perform best with a frequent mowing schedule, and tend to get bogged down in gnarly grass. Corded models work best on lawns with minimal obstructions. Rechargeable models operate for an hour or so before needing a recharge, but the risk of running over the extension cord is eliminated. However, corded models use less electricity than rechargeable models.

Gas-powered models generally have more power than electric models and are available as walk-behind or riding types. Walk-behind mowers can be push types that move forward at the speed you are pushing, or they can be self-propelled, which means they have powered wheels that propel the machine forward. Walk-behind mowers are good for small to mid-sized lawns, and large lawns if you like exercise. The larger horsepower, walk-behind mowers rarely bog down in thick, dry grass. A self-propelled mower should have a range of ground speeds to accommodate different lawn conditions; slower speeds may be needed for thick, lush lawns. Riding mowers with a wide cutting deck are good for large lawns.

It is interesting to note that a study by Swedish scientists suggests that the air pollution from cutting grass for an hour with a gas-powered lawn mower is about the same as driving 100 miles in your average car. That is a lot of emissions just to mow the lawn.

Vertical mowers

Vertical mowers, or verticutters, are used for slicing vertically through the grass. Verticutters are used for thatch removal, light turf cultivation for minor renovation, and to slice stolons of stoloniferous grasses to promote vegetative reproduction. Some types of verticutters are known as power rakes, which are used specifically for thatch reduction and removal, especially during spring and fall lawn clean-up.

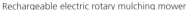
Rechargeable electric rotary mulching mower

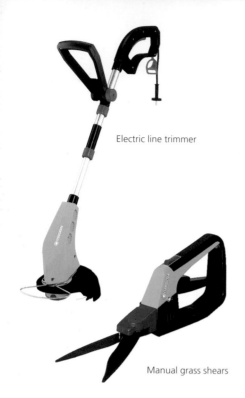

Electric line trimmer

Manual grass shears

Line trimmers

Line trimmers come in gas and electric models. Some electric models come with rechargeable batteries for cord-free operation. Electric models are the most environmentally friendly line trimmers. Line trimmers can be hand-held or they can be worn with a strap

Using an electric line trimmer

or harness. Some larger, gas-powered models come with wheels and resemble lawn mowers. The cutting is done by a fast-spinning nylon line or a solid cutting blade. Some brands of line trimmers come with attachments so the line trimmer can be converted into a hedge trimmer, a pole pruner, a power broom, a blower or a mini-cultivator. If you are considering a line trimmer, make sure it is comfortable for you to use and relatively easy to install new trimming line.

Grass shears

Grass shears work like scissors. They come in short-handled models that require you to bend down to use them, and long-handled models that can be used in a standing position. Some new models of grass shears are rechargeable electric models that operate the same as haircutting shears. You still have to bend down to use them, though.

Environmentally, the best trimmer choice is hand-powered grass shears. Grass shears do a good job, plus you get to examine your turfgrass close-up, and you get some exercise.

Tools for Edging

Lawns look really good with nice, straight, trimmed edges. Edgers can be manually operated hand models or gas-powered models. Some hand models are used like shovels and come with a thin, sharp blade and a long handle. The blade is pushed vertically into the turfgrass to create a straight edge along the turfgrass. Other hand-powered edgers have a wheel at the end of a long handle, with cutting teeth along the side edge of the wheel. This type of edger is pushed along the edge of the turfgrass, cutting a nice, clean edge. Hand-powered edgers are the best environmental choice. Gas-powered models have a solid metal blade that spins vertically. They can be walk-behind models or they can resemble line trimmers. Powered models are pushed or guided along the edge of the turfgrass.

Tools for Fertilizing

You will need a way to apply fertilizer to your lawn. The fertilizer you use will determine the best method of application.

Granular fertilizers, such as corn gluten meal, can be applied with a rotary spreader, a drop spreader or by hand. Drop spreaders provide the highest degree of uniform application for granular products. Rotary spreaders can apply the same volume of granular product much quicker than a drop spreader. These two types of spreaders are very easy to operate. Ensure the spreader you use is easy to adjust and calibrate.

Liquid fertilizers, such as compost tea, will need to be sprayed onto the lawn surface. Sprayers come in models you carry or set on the ground while spraying or models you can wear on your back. Sprayers operate by manual pumping to increase air pressure inside the tank. The air pressure forces the liquid out the spray nozzle when the trigger mechanism is pressed. Applying liquid fertilizers is an exacting task— the pressure inside the spray tank, your ground speed and the speed at which you pass the spray wand over the ground need to remain as consistent as possible. Sprayers are also much harder to calibrate than granular fertilizer spreaders. Fortunately, when spraying good-quality compost tea, there is not the need to be as exact as with other liquid fertilizers.

Rotary spreaders work best for granular fertilizer products.

Bulk organic fertilizers, such as compost, are best spread by hand for small- to medium-sized lawns (see Simple Fertility Program, p. 97). For this you need a scoop or a grain shovel (or any shovel that you can handle easily), a garden rake and a push broom with medium-stiff bristles. Drop spreaders and rotary spreaders are not the best for spreading compost because of the bulky nature of the compost. Very large lawns can be done with a rented top dresser, a machine used on golf courses and sports fields.

Tools for Seasonal Maintenance

These tools you will only use once or twice a year, or even every couple of years, and are available at tool rental places. These are the tools you see the lawn care companies using for spring and fall maintenance.

Aerators

There are a few different types of aerators available—core aerators, solid tine (shatter time) aerators, aerators that inject water and a liquid aerator.

Gas-powered, drum-type core aerator

Aerators that remove a core (or plug) of soil do the best job. Only core aerators provide the opportunity to introduce amendment material directly into the rootzone. These are available in gas-powered models and as hand tools. Gas-powered models are much quicker than hand tool models, but much less friendly for the environment. Gas-powered models can be a drum type that has hollow tines fixed to the outside of a drum that spoons out soil cores as it rolls along, or a camshaft- or crankshaft-driven type that uses mechanical action to plunge the tines into the soil.

High-quality manual core aerator
(from Accuproducts International)

Camshaft- or crankshaft-driven aerators are far more efficient than drum types. Hand aerators are a good environmental choice. Once again, using the human-powered tool lets you closely examine your lawn and get some exercise. The bonus for us lazy types is that you only have to do it, at most, once a year.

Solid-tine aerators have solid tines that poke holes into the soil, often shattering the soil around the holes. This type of aerator does not disrupt the lawn surface and can be used as a temporary fix for compacted soil. The tines can be narrow and pin-like, or can resemble large, triangular teeth. Those with large teeth are often referred to as slicers.

It is best if the soil is a little drier when using solid tines for aeration. The impact of the tines will shatter the soil through the rootzone. It leaves the soil a little fluffy, but a single pass with a water-filled roller will help smooth the surface.

However, solid tine aeration can cause injury to the roots, and you are more likely to develop a hardpan layer at the depth the tines penetrate. Solid tine aeration does not provide the same opportunity for adding amendments beneath the turfgrass cover.

A third type of aerator works by injecting water to loosen the soil. Large, gas-powered models inject water in pulses at very high pressure, which shatters the soil profile to create pore space and relieve compaction. Hand models are available that attach to a hose and are easily stepped into the ground. Water is fed through the tines to loosen the soil and create pore space. This type of aerator is good for spot-watering dry areas.

One risk with using mechanical aerators is that you can develop a hardpan layer at the depth of the tines. This can be alleviated by using deep-tine aerators that penetrate 12–16" into the soil. Deep-tine aerators usually have solid tines, but units with hollow tines are available. Deep-tine aeration is usually unnecessary for home lawns.

Also available is a liquid product, called Aerify!, that penetrates into the soil, breaking apart the bonds that hold together clay particles and other compacted soil particles, and also stimulating biological processes. This product is available in the U.S. (www.natureslawn.com).

Thatch rake attachment (from Gardena Combisystem hand tools)

Power rakes

A power rake is a type of vertical mower that is used for thatch removal and can be used to break up aeration cores. These power rakes are gas-powered units that roughly resemble lawn mowers. The types that have knives or blades do the best cutting job. There are power rake attachments for rotary lawn mowers, but these tend to do more damage to the turf than regular power rakes. There are also environmentally friendly, human-powered thatch rakes that have a specially designed rake head and a long handle. These rakes do a good job and there is the exercise thing again. A standard garden rake can also be used as a thatch rake.

Hand Tools

It is important to have a few hand tools to aid with your lawn maintenance. Minimally, these include a grain shovel, a garden rake, a fan rake, a spade, a round-nosed shovel, a dandelion popper, a garden fork (potato fork) and a push broom. With these hand tools you can accomplish many of your turfgrass maintenance tasks. A wheelbarrow, which is handy for moving bulk material such as compost and soil, can be rented or borrowed.

Tool Maintenance

It is important to properly maintain your tools. This means keeping them clean, sharpened (if a blade is involved), tuned-up (if you have gas-powered equipment), and properly adjusted or calibrated. Your tools will last longer and perform better with regular maintenance.

The hand tools you use for lawn maintenance can be used to maintain your entire landscape.

Turfgrass Nutrition

AN ACTIVELY GROWING TURFGRASS PLANT IS 75–85% WATER. THE REST OF the plant is composed of organic compounds made from 16 essential elements necessary for healthy growth and completion of the turfgrass lifecycle. All plants require these 16 elements in various proportions. Carbon, hydrogen and oxygen are the most abundant elements in plants; these elements are obtained from the atmosphere and from water. The other 13 elements are absorbed from the soil by the plant roots. Nutrients can also be absorbed through the leaves and stems. The leaves and stems are the major uptake routes for carbon dioxide, but most other mineral and water absorption is through the roots.

The nutrients most used by turfgrass are nitrogen, potassium and phosphorous, in that order. When you look at a bag of fertilizer, there are three numbers separated by hyphens (e.g., 7-2-2, 12-3-8), which represent the percentage of nitrogen, phosphorous and potassium, respectively, in the fertilizer formulation. For example, if the fertilizer is a 7-2-2 formulation then it has 7% nitrogen. If the bag weighs 22 lbs, the actual amount of nitrogen in the bag is approximately 1½ pounds.

Forms of nitrogen and potassium existing in the soil that are readily available for use by the turfgrass are used up quickly or they leach into the lower layers of the soil out of reach of the roots. You may need to add these nutrients in the form of an organic fertilizer. There is often enough phosphorous in the soil, but it may be unavailable to the plant if the soil pH is too high. It is important to remember that the soil pH affects the availability of nutrients. The amount and diversity of soil microorganisms also affects the amount and availability of nutrients. Add fertilizers based on a soil test and foodweb assay.

Turfgrass can also absorb more minerals than it needs for growth. Small amounts of at least 40 other minerals and elements have been found in turfgrass tissues. Depending on the amount of these other elements in the soil, turfgrass nutrition can be adversely affected. These other elements can interfere with the uptake of the essential elements, or they can be present in large enough quantities that they are toxic to the plant.

The Non-organic Fertilizing Method

Plants have grown and thrived for millions of years without being fertilized. However, much of our effort with turfgrass fertility in recent times has been through the use of non-organic techniques that focus solely on providing the plant with what it needs, with no thought about the rest of the organisms that live in, around and on the turfgrass. The non-organic fertilizing method is to add nutrients in forms that are readily available to the plant. Fertilizer is applied to the turfgrass based on a soil test that shows the amount and form of nutrients, the soil pH and the amount of salts in the existing soil.

Dr. James B. Beard, President and Chief Scientist of the International Sports Turf Institute and Professor Emeritus of Turfgrass Science at Texas A&M University, has written:

It is critical to educate the general public that the darkest green turf, which many people strive for, is not in fact the healthiest turf. A medium green turf with a moderate growth rate will have the deepest root system with less thatching, reduced disease and insect problems, and increased tolerance to environmental stresses such as heat, drought, cold, and wear. (*Journal of Environmental Quality,* May 1994.)

For many years now, those of us involved in the care of turfgrass lawns and landscapes have happily applied bag after bag of chemical fertilizer to get the nice, dark green lawn that is the envy of the neighbors. Turfgrass may appear healthy after applying a chemical fertilizer, but the effect of that chemical fertilizer on the soil is a different matter. The salt content of chemical fertilizers is toxic to microbial life, and the nutrients applied may disrupt the balance of soil organisms. Continued use of chemical fertilizers depletes the soil of microorganisms and begins a cycle of chemical dependency and problems.

The cycle of dependency arises from the fact that you have disrupted or removed all the organisms that trap and cycle nutrients in the soil. At that point, the turfgrass depends on the chemical fertilizers for its nutritional needs. As these artificial resources are used up by the plants or leach out of the soil, the plants' vigor declines, and you have to apply another shot of chemical fertilizers.

The disruption of the soil microorganism profile makes lawns more prone to various problems, such as weeds, disease, thatch and drought. When the microbial profile is out of balance, it can cause nutrient flushes in the soil that favor weed growth. There can also be an increase in plant diseases, because the organisms that usually keep the disease organisms in check are not present. Thatch buildup occurs when the organisms that consume dead plant matter are missing or out of balance. Drought damage can happen when the soil structure is not maintained by a healthy population of soil microorganisms. The soil is easily compacted when it lacks good structure, and this compacted soil prevents the roots from drawing water from deeper sources. The roots may also be void of the symbiotic mycorrhizal fungi necessary for healthy turf growth.

The current method of fertilizing our lawns has disrupted the balance of life in the soil, and we see problems on lawns as a result of our maintenance practices. If we can switch our thinking and practices from feeding the plants to feeding and keeping the soil healthy, we will keep all life healthy, including the turfgrass.

Soil and Nutrition

Plants and the soil they grow in have a unique relationship—many important plant functions go on underground. Soil holds air, water, nutrients, organic matter and a variety of beneficial organisms. Plants depend upon these resources for their nutritional needs, and their roots use the soil as an anchor. In turn, plants influence soil development by breaking down large clods with their roots. They increase soil fertility by releasing by-products during their growth and by being recycled by soil microorganisms when they die.

The mineral portion of soil is made up of particles of different sizes. Sand particles are the largest. Sand has lots of air space and doesn't compact easily, so water drains quickly out of sandy soil and nutrients are quickly washed away. Clay particles are the smallest, visible only through a microscope. Water penetrates clay very slowly and drains very slowly. Clay holds the most nutrients, but it compacts easily. Silt particles are smaller than sand particles but larger than clay particles. Most soil is made up of a mixture of different particle sizes. Soils with a balanced mix of these three particle sizes are called loams.

The pH of soil is its measure of acidity or alkalinity. A pH of 7 is neutral; higher numbers (up to 14) indicate alkaline conditions, and lower numbers (down to 0) indicate acidic conditions.

Although some plants prefer acid or alkaline soils, most of the turfgrass species we use grow best in a mid-range pH of between 5.5 and 7.0, with an optimal pH of 6.5.

The organic matter portion of the soil includes living and dead components. The dead components are the residues, metabolites and waste products of plants, animals and microorganisms. The living components are composed of bacteria, fungi, nematodes, protozoa, arthropods (that's insects, spiders and their kin for us common folk) and earthworms. These organisms decompose organic compounds, including plant and animal residues and wastes, pesticides and other pollutants. They trap and store nitrogen and other nutrients in their bodies, and they produce hormones that plants use. Their activities enhance soil structure for better air and water movement into the soil and less runoff. They compete with and prey on plant pests, and they provide food for above-ground animals. The living soil organisms, the dead organic components, the plants and the aboveground animals make up what is known as the soil foodweb.

The Soil Foodweb

It is important for you to gain a basic understanding of the organisms that live in the soil and what processes they perform in the soil, so that you will understand how our current turf maintenance and installation practices affect these organisms and their processes. Dr. Elaine Ingham has researched and gathered information from many sources about the immense diversity of soil organisms and the roles they play. Some of the information included in this book is taken (with permission) from the *Soil Biology Primer* (Soil and Water Conservation Society and the USDA Natural Resources Conservation Service, 2000) and from Dr. Ingham's website www.soilfoodweb.com. The

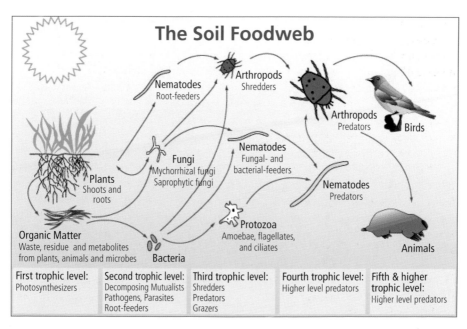

The Soil Foodweb

information applies to everywhere in the world where you find soil and plants. The primer and website go into far greater detail than the information presented here.

At the base of the soil foodweb are the photosynthesizers (plants, moss, algae and photosynthetic bacteria) that use sunshine to convert atmospheric carbon dioxide to useable compounds they need for their structure and growth. As these organisms progress through their life cycle, they add organic matter to the soil in the form of dead cells, plant residues and metabolites produced during the organisms' growth. Most other soil organisms get their carbon and energy from eating plants and their residues, other organisms and waste by-products.

The next level up is composed of bacteria, saprophytic and mycorrhizal fungi and root feeding nematodes. The organisms at this level are decomposers, mutualistic organisms, pathogens, parasites and root feeders.

Decomposers are bacteria and fungi that break down simple and complex residues. As they break down residues they retain nutrients in their bodies, while binding themselves to soil particles. They prevent nutrient loss from the soil that would be caused by leaching and they create new organic compounds in the form of cells and waste by-products that are a source of food for the higher levels in the web. They create compounds that help bind soil into stable aggregates, as do fungal strands known as hyphae. Some forms of bacteria at this level convert nitrogen into different forms. These bacterial and fungal decomposers compete for space and nutrients or inhibit the growth of disease-causing organisms.

Mutualistic organisms enhance growth and protect roots from disease-causing organisms. Mycorrhizal fungi form associations with plant roots that help provide the plant with nutrients and water in exchange for carbon compounds from the plant. Some bacteria, such as the type found in association with the roots of legumes such as white clover, have the ability to use atmospheric nitrogen in their growth. The nitrogen is later made available to the plants and to the other soil organisms when the bacteria decompose or are eaten.

Pathogens and parasites promote disease. When the foodweb is out of balance, these organisms can cause much damage to our plants. The silver lining is that some of these organisms are parasites of, or cause disease in, disease-causing organisms.

Root feeders, such as nematodes and insect larvae, eat plant roots and can cause substantial damage to lawns and other plants.

The third level of the soil foodweb contains arthropods, nematodes and protozoa. The protozoa are divided into three groups including amoeba, flagellates and ciliates. The organisms at this level are grazers, shredders and some low-level predators.

Grazers of bacteria are the protozoa and nematodes, and grazers of fungi are the nematodes and microarthropods. The nutrients trapped in the bacteria and fungi are not available to the plants until the grazers eat the bacteria and fungi. When eating bacteria and fungi, grazers release plant-available nutrients, control many root-feeding or disease-causing pests, and stimulate and control the bacterial and fungal populations.

Shredders include macroarthropods

Turfgrasses thrive with a bacterial-dominated foodweb. Trees and shrubs require a fungal-dominated foodweb.

and earthworms that break down residues, such as plant litter, and enhance soil structure by burrowing through the soil and producing fecal pellets. The shredders provide habitat for bacteria in their guts and in their fecal pellets. Earthworms are generalist feeders that consume many different soil organisms and residues.

The fourth level of the soil foodweb includes larger predatory arthropods and predatory nematodes. **The fifth level** contains mice, voles, birds and other above-ground animals. The organisms at these two levels control the populations of the organisms at lower levels in the soil foodweb. Larger organisms, including earthworms, improve soil structure through their burrowing actions and by passing soil through their guts. Larger organisms also help distribute the smaller organisms by carrying them long distances.

The organisms that comprise the soil foodweb help develop good soil structure by binding soil particles together and creating air channels and passages

through the soil as they search for food. Both plants and foodweb organisms need good air and water movement in the soil for good health. Soil with good structure allows excess water to drain, and also helps to hold water when the soil starts to dry out.

Soil organisms are not present in the soil all the time. Many soil organisms do not grow old and die, but go dormant when environmental conditions are not favorable for active growth. Natural disturbances, including freezing and thawing, excessive wetness, drought, fire and soil compaction, and human disturbances such as excessive cultivation, use of chemical fertilizers and use of pesticides, can kill these organisms.

Feeding the Soil

The key to a successful fertility program is to feed the soil, not the plant. Soils are dynamic ecosystems containing many thousands of soil organisms that work in harmony with each other and the plants. Any practice that disrupts the balance of the soil ecosystem can mean problems for the plants. If you take proper care of your soil, it will produce good-quality turfgrass.

Soils often contain all the nutritional requirements for turfgrass. However, these elements are often bound to other elements in the soil or trapped in the bodies of soil microorganisms and are unavailable to the plant. Enhancing the soil with all kinds of beneficial bacteria, fungi and other microorganisms helps free up the tightly bound elements as the organisms eat and are eaten, releasing nutrients into the soil in forms the plants can use. Large populations of microorganisms in the soil can trap and use much of the available nutritional elements they need for their growth. Enhancing the beneficial soil organism population also helps fight disease and insect attacks, and reduces the fertilizer and water needs of the turfgrass.

There are hundreds of soil types and soil distribution patterns. It is important for you to know the soil type of your property. Taking the soil you have and amending it with good-quality compost is a step in the right direction. But first, take a step that is too often ignored by gardeners—have your soil tested.

There are two types of soil tests that will let you know exactly what is happening in your soil. A standard soil test measures pH level, nutrient content (amount and forms) and how much organic matter is present. Standard soil tests will provide suggestions on how to alter the soil's characteristics (pH, mineral content, percentage of organic matter) to grow the plants you want to grow. The types of turfgrass we use for our lawns grow best in well-drained, moisture-holding loam with a pH in the range of 5.5–7.3.

The other type of test is a foodweb assay. This test counts total and active bacteria, total and active fungi, numbers and types of protozoa, and numbers and types of nematodes. It also assesses whether the sample is aerobic

Healthy soil and a healthy soil foodweb benefit the entire garden.

or anaerobic, identifies the kind and amount of beneficial mycorrhizal colonization on the roots (if you include roots in the sample), and determines how much of the plant surface is covered with microorganisms. The foodweb assay will provide suggestions on how to bring the soil life into the balance and diversity needed to grow the plants you want to grow. The turfgrass species we use prefer a soil with an equal balance of fungi and bacteria.

Standard soil tests and foodweb assays cost relatively little compared to the information they provide. Contact the labs for directions on how to take and submit samples. Standard soil tests done by accredited labs give more accurate, comprehensive results and better recommendations than the results you will get from do-it-yourself soil-testing kits. Both standard soil tests and foodweb assays provide useful information, and both are necessary for planning your turfgrass fertility program. Always inform the labs of the plants you intend to grow; the labs can provide specific recommendations on how to best amend the soil to grow those plants. Have the standard soil test done first, as it is important that the technicians doing the foodweb assay know the chemistry of the soil.

Modern agriculture has done much to destroy the beneficial organisms in the soil and on plant surfaces. Pest-control methods were designed to kill pest organisms, often with toxic chemicals. In other words, pesticides kill things. This method has an unfortunate side effect of severely damaging or killing all the beneficial soil organisms and those organisms that protect plant surfaces. Another unfortunate side effect is that disease-causing organisms rebound faster than beneficial organisms from toxic chemical applications, compounding the problems. So modern agriculture (and horticulture, which includes turf management) has severely depleted the populations of soil organisms and has selected disease-causing organisms over

beneficial organisms. From this perspective it is not hard to see why we have so many insect pest and disease problems.

The 12-step soil repair process

Now having learned about the practices that have caused serious soil problems and harmed the soil foodweb, we must go about the task of repair. Fortunately, it is possible to repair the foodweb and bring it into the correct balance to grow healthy plants. Dr. Ingham has developed a 12-step process for repairing and enhancing the soil foodweb. The process involves adding back the soil microorganisms in a certain order to re-establish the foodweb. The 12-step process to repair your soil is based on the results of your soil foodweb assay. The desired range for each type of soil microorganism is given in the report and is based on the type of plants you are growing, the soil type, the climate and the season of growth. Below is a brief outline of the 12 steps. I encourage you to visit Dr. Ingham's website or get a copy of the *Soil Biology Primer*.

Step One in Dr. Ingham's process is to make sure there is adequate bacterial diversity and activity. A diversity of species ensures the full range of nutrient

cycling. No one bacterial group can cycle all the nutrients needed. If the level of bacterial diversity is low, then bacteria can be added by using a healthy, aerobic compost, compost tea or commercial inoculum. If using commercial inoculum, look for maximum diversity in the bacterial species. Avoid inocula containing anaerobic bacteria.

If the bacterial level is too high and out of balance for the turfgrass, add fungi to bring the system back to balance.

Step Two is to feed the bacteria, if bacterial activity is too low. Plant roots often supply the simple sugars, proteins and carbohydrates that bacteria eat, but that may not be enough. Add a diversity of bacterial foods, such as molasses, fish emulsion or fruit juices to increase growth rates and population. The greater the diversity of bacterial foods added, the greater the diversity of species of bacteria that will thrive.

Step Three is to ensure adequate fungal diversity. This critical step cannot occur without the first step of building good bacterial populations and diversity. No one fungal group can cycle all the nutrients needed, and a diversity of fungal species is needed as well. Beneficial fungi can be added

Naturally maintained lawns allow the soil foodweb to grow and diversify.

Mass of fungal strands

Fungal hyphae

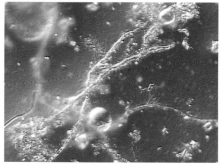

Fungi and bacteria

Step Four is to feed the beneficial fungi, if fungal activity is too low. These fungi consume the more complex carbon substrates such as sloughed root cells and dead plant tissue; generally the tougher, woodier plant parts. Fish hydrolysate, fish oils, complex sugars, amino sugars, complex proteins, soybean meal, humic acids, fulvic acids, wood, sawdust, bark, paper and cardboard can all be used as fungal food sources, but using a diversity of foods is important. The greater the diversity of fungal foods, the greater the diversity of fungal species that will grow. Fungi are good at condensing organic matter into complex forms, such as converting fulvic to humic acids.

Soil tests will often indicate that some nutrient is in low supply, but merely by adding the appropriate bacterial or fungal species, these organisms will convert plant-unavailable nutrients into plant-available forms. Diversity is the key, however, as well as feeding that diverse set of species so they will perform their functions.

Bacteria and fungi hold nutrients in the soil. They incorporate nutrients into their body parts, fastening themselves to soil particles (or any surface) with glues and strands, provided these glues and strands are not destroyed. This prevents nutrients from leaching deeper into the soil than the roots can reach, and into groundwater.

back to the soil by using a healthy, aerobic compost or compost tea. You can add some soil from the humus layer in forest soils, but be very careful not to damage or overly deplete the resource. If the fungal level is high and out of balance for the turfgrass, add bacteria to restore the balance.

Beneficial fungi require aerobic conditions. If your soil is compacted or overly wet, the beneficial fungi may not survive. Anaerobic conditions tend to favor disease-causing organisms.

Step Five is to make sure the roots of your desired plants are colonized by mycorrhiza. Mycorrhizal fungi are needed by some plants, including turfgrass, are absolutely critical for other plants and are probably detrimental for other plants. Early successional plant species, such as weeds, mustards and kale, do not require mycorrhizal fungi and may be harmed by it. Ensuring good mycorrhizal colonization of your turfgrass roots may help keep weeds at bay.

If the mycorrhizal colonization is low, or less than the desired range, you will have to add the appropriate mycorrhizal spores to the soil near the plant roots. Not all mycorrhiza are the same. Different species and different types of those species colonize certain plants; make sure you have the kind needed for your plants. When adding mycorrhizal spores, be sure the spores can reach the root system of the plant.

Grasses and annual plants need vesicular-arbuscular mycorrhiza (VAM), coniferous evergreen trees require ectomycorrhizal colonization, and blueberries and their relatives need ericoid mycorrhizal fungi.

To add mycorrhiza to lawns, add VAM spores to compost, then use this mix to topdress the lawn after aeration. To add mycorrhiza when seeding a new lawn, apply VAM spores to the soil with the seed or very shortly after.

Feeding the lawn with humic acid compounds aids in good mycorrhizal colonization of the plant roots. Weather, severe drought, floods, burns and compaction can reduce colonization.

Steps Six, Seven and Eight ensure your soil has adequate numbers of protozoa in order to cycle nutrients and to build air passageways. Flagellates, amoebae and ciliates are the three groups of protozoa. Nutrients tied up by bacteria cannot be used by the plants; protozoa eat bacteria to release nutrients into the soil for plants to use. Protozoa also help build larger soil pores by pushing aggregates around as they search for their bacterial prey.

If the protozoa are too low in number, the nutrients remain tied up in the bacteria and fungi. An inorganic fertilizer will have to be added in order to supply nutrients to the plant. This is expensive and a large proportion of these nutrients will likely be lost from the soil, either by leaching or by volatilization. Protozoa can be reintroduced to the soil by adding good-quality compost or compost tea, or a commercial inoculum.

If the protozoa are within the desired range, reductions in fertilizer applications should be possible. If protozoa numbers are extremely high, or the different groups are very unbalanced, then nutrient cycling will vary, with periods of high nutrient flushes that may favor weeds.

To keep the protozoa healthy, feed them bacteria (see steps one and two).

Steps Nine, Ten and Eleven are to ensure there are adequate numbers of nematodes of the right kinds to help nutrient cycling, and to build water and air passages in the soil. You need bacterial-feeding nematodes, fungal-feeding nematodes and predatory nematodes. Bacterial-feeding and fungal-feeding nematodes make nutrients available to plants when they are active in the plants' rootzone. Bacterial-feeding and fungal-feeding nematodes also interfere with the ability of harmful root-feeding nematodes to find the plant roots. Predatory nematodes feed on protozoa and other nematodes, including root-feeding nematodes. The more beneficial nematodes there are, the more nutrient cycling is occurring. Beneficial nematodes can be added to the soil by using good-quality compost or compost tea.

If your soil has earthworms, it has a healthy soil foodweb.

Step Twelve is to ensure there are earthworms and/or microarthropods present in the soil. When these organisms are present, then the full foodweb is present. They can be added, but many just show up when the rest of the foodweb is present.

If the numbers of individual soil organisms are adequate, plant health can almost be guaranteed, because all the processes will be functioning.

Repairing any individual group of soil organisms is as simple as adding the organisms back to the soil. They will reproduce as long as an adequate food supply is available. The more organisms and food for the organisms you add, the quicker the soil will return to full health. If your soil has toxic chemicals or undecomposed litter material, these materials have to be eaten by the soil organisms before beginning the 12-step program.

How to add bacterial and fungal foods

Ideally, we should emulate nature by placing bacterial and fungal foods on the soil surface. On established lawns, surface applications are the only way to add these foods to the soil. The foodweb organisms will incorporate the foods into the soil.

When doing lawn renovation or re-establishment, mixing these foods into the top layer of soil causes greater bacterial activity. However, any soil disturbance, such as rototilling or compaction, kills many soil organisms and disrupts the soil structure. Keep tillage to a minimum.

When adding bacterial and fungal foods, make sure that a mineral crust does not develop. A mineral crust will decrease water infiltration, water-holding capacity and root penetration.

One cubic yard of compost is more than enough to fertilize an average home lawn.

How can I tell if the soil foodweb is working?

During periods of optimal moisture and temperature (spring, and fall in some areas), if there is a diversity of soil microorganisms and they are healthy, bacterial foods should disappear in 2 to 9 weeks and fungal foods should disappear in 6 to 16 weeks. If, after a month or more of warm weather, you can still identify the bacterial and fungal foods you have applied, then some part of the soil foodweb is lacking and needs to be added. In other words, if you still see compost on the soil surface, or a sugary goo on the foliage, then the foodweb isn't working yet.

It is a good idea to get a foodweb assay done, at least annually for the first couple of years as you switch to natural methods from chemical methods, to make sure you have the correct numbers and diversity of soil organisms for the plants you are growing. Monitoring the foodweb at different times provides different results. Fall testing allows you to see if your maintenance practices for the year were effective, and lets you deal with any current problems and to plan

management strategies for the next season. Organic matter additions in the fall decompose rapidly during the winter, even under the snow, if the soil foodweb is healthy. The heat produced by the metabolic process helps warm the soil in spring. Testing the soil foodweb in the spring will let you know if the beneficial soil microorganisms are growing, or if problems are developing.

Spreading compost manually with grain shovel.

Simple Fertility Program

The following is a basic fertility program for home lawns that will help you switch from a chemically intensive lawn to an organic lawn. You can begin this program in spring or fall, once your soil has been tested and recommendations for amendments given.

Spring

Spring turf work can begin once the grass is actively growing, usually in April or May, but it can begin earlier depending on the weather. After you have dethatched (if necessary) and aerated the lawn, spread a ½" thick layer of good-quality compost over the entire lawn and work it in with a push broom. Apply only ¼" of compost if you have not aerated. If you are overseeding and/or adding amendments (per soil test and foodweb recommendations), do the overseeding and amending before you apply the compost.

You may still need to use some fertilizer as you switch from chemical to organic maintenance. Fertilize with a granular organic fertilizer according to the instructions on the package label and based on a soil test. Use only organic fertilizers as they help build life in the soil. Use caution when selecting commercial organic fertilizers to ensure the ingredients are indeed natural and organic.

Fall

If you are applying a commercial organic fertilizer only once a year, fall is the best time to do it. Microbial activity slows but does not stop in the winter. Soil microorganisms have all winter to break down fall-applied fertilizer. This makes nutrients available to the plants in spring, when plant growth resumes. You can apply fall fertilizer when the turfgrass is going dormant, usually around late September. Aeration can also be done in early fall (September) provided the turfgrass is still actively growing. Apply ½" of compost if aerating and ¼" of compost if not aerating.

Ongoing

Leave the grass clippings on the lawn even if you don't have a mulching mower. Earthworms and beneficial microorganisms will break down the clippings, returning valuable nutrients and enzymes to the soil.

Allow clover to grow in your lawn. Clover and turfgrass grow well together. Clover will not outcompete the turfgrass if the turfgrass is healthy. Clover provides free nutrition to your lawn and soil, anywhere from ¼ to ⅓ of the turfgrass requirements depending on the species grown. A 10–20% population of white clover spread evenly throughout the lawn is acceptable.

Sprinkling compost into a tight area.

Lawn covered in compost

Fertilizer Choices

We now have a wide range of commercial organic fertilizers available for use on turfgrass, and these often contain ingredients that feed both soil bacteria and soil fungi. Granular organic fertilizers release their nutrients slowly. Soil microorganisms must break down the granules before the nutrients are available to the turfgrass. This provides a steady supply of nutrients for the lawn, eliminating the flushes of growth that are often associated with chemical fertilizers. Liquid organic fertilizers are a little faster acting as the material is already in a water solution, but they

Use a rake to spread out thick spots.

still need to be acted upon by the soil microorganisms. Nurseries and garden centers now carry a good selection of organic turf fertilizers.

Natural organic materials used for fertilizer include activated or processed sewage sludge, animal and vegetable tankage (dried plant and animal residues, often with the fat and gelatin content removed), manure, soybean meal and cottonseed meal. These can be single-product formulations, such as straight bone meal, or they can be combinations of various ingredients. Many of the new organic fertilizers on the market for turfgrass are combination products, which provide a wide range of bacterial and fungal foods. There is an organic commercial turfgrass fertilizer with mycorrhizae (Myke™) available. Because these natural organic materials differ in their composition, they break down at different rates. All of the natural organic materials release nitrogen at slower rates than do the quickly available, chemical nitrogen sources.

Advantages of using organic fertilizers

Organic fertilizers release nitrogen slowly, with less chance of the nitrogen leaching through the soil or running off the surface, and less chance of fertilizer burn than with many chemical fertilizers. Organic fertilizers can be applied infrequently at high rates. They help to increase the soil microorganism population and activities, resulting in better water-holding capacity, better aeration, lower disease incidence and less thatch accumulation. Organic fertilizers have a low salt content, and are safe to apply during hot weather. Organically fertilized lawns grow slower than chemically fertilized lawns, thus requiring less mowing. Also, as your turfgrass ecosystem and soil food-web come back into balance, your fertilizer needs will decrease.

Disadvantages of using organic fertilizers

Although the following points are listed as disadvantages, they truly are just points to be aware of when using organic fertilizers. Organic fertilizers may be more expensive per pound of nitrogen than chemical fertilizers. The low nitrogen levels in organic fertilizer may not provide all the nitrogen the turfgrass needs, and large amounts may need to be applied. Organic fertilizers need to be broken down by microorganisms first before the nutrients become available to the plants. You don't see the quick green-up that you do with chemical fertilizers. Also, the nutrients from organic fertilizers are not released as quickly in the cool seasons of spring and fall, as the soil microorganisms are not as active in cool weather.

Work compost into the lawn with a push broom.

The compost should be barely visible.

Some organic fertilizers may contain weed seeds. Some have a high carbon content and may tie up plant-available nitrogen. Some organic fertilizers are bulky to transport and store, and some may have an offensive smell.

Grasscycling

Grass is the only crop that we grow of which the parts we harvest are the parts we throw away. Those grass clippings that you spend so much time bagging up and paying to get hauled away can do a lot more good if left on the lawn. One good reason is that those grass clippings can provide 25–50% of the nutritional needs of your lawn, depending on the species of turfgrass you have in your lawn. The process of returning the grass clippings to the lawn rather than bagging them up is known as grasscycling or mulch mowing.

- Grasscycling works best when the turfgrass is properly mowed (see Mowing, p. 59). Grasscycling is easiest when you mow with a mulching mower, but a regular mower can provide the same effect. When using a regular mower keep the blades sharp, mow more often, especially in spring and fall when the turfgrass is actively growing, and mow only when the grass is dry.
- Grasscycling does not cause thatch build-up (see Thatch, p. 73). Grass clippings decompose rapidly.

A freshly fertilized lawn

- Grasscycling does not spread disease in lawns (see Disease, p. 130). Poor maintenance practices are the main cause of disease spread.

Compost

Compost is used to add foodweb organisms to the soil. When compost is made correctly, it will contain bacteria, fungi, protozoa, nematodes and often microarthropods. Compost provides a food source for soil foodweb organisms. Compost can help add structure elements to soil; it often contains substances such as clay, bits of wood and other fibrous materials that enhance the physical structure and help provide air channels and passages.

All composts are not the same, and compost for use on turfgrass must meet certain parameters. Peter Landschoot, Associate Professor of Turfgrass Science at Penn State College of Agricultural Sciences, provides us with the parameters of what makes good-quality compost.

> **Compost tea**, if made from manure compost and not made carefully enough, can create problems of toxicity for plants and a chance for E. coli to develop. High-tech, quality controlled, aerobically activated compost teas are just coming on the market, fully alive and very perishable, but worth the price.

- Good-quality compost is light and crumbly (with no visible or identifiable debris, such as pieces of wood), and looks like dark brown topsoil.
- To topdress existing turfgrass, use ⅜" screened compost. Larger particle sizes are acceptable for mixing into the soil.
- Good-quality compost has an earthy smell. Do not purchase or use compost that has any funny or foul odor. It was noted by Dr. Ingham that good compost should smell more like mushrooms than like earth.
- Properly made compost will contain very few (if any) weed seeds. If possible, it is a good idea to visit the location where the compost is made to see if there is an abundance of weeds there.
- Compost with 30–50% moisture content is easy to work with and mixes well into soil. Compost with greater than 60% moisture content is heavy, hard to handle and tends to clump when you try to mix it into the soil. Compost with less than 20% moisture content floats on top of the soil when trying to incorporate it, blows away easily in a medium to stiff wind (which can leave a dust film on cars, houses, plants, etc.), and may get into your eyes and lungs when using it.
- The ash content should be less than 30%, with the better compost containing less ash.
- Good compost will have a carbon to nitrogen ratio of 30:1 (C:N) or less. The more carbon present in the compost, the more nitrogen is tied up in the decomposition process.
- Compost should have a pH of 6.0–8.0, with a pH of 7 being ideal.
- Some compost may contain more metals than other compost does.

Check that the types and amounts of metal in the compost are below health guidelines.

• Check for salt content and type of salt, as some salts are more damaging than others (i.e., sodium) and some turfgrass species are more sensitive to some forms of salts. For compost with a higher salt concentration, the salt can be leached with fresh water immediately after application. Salt-heavy compost does more damage when surface applied than when incorporated.

Also noted by Dr. Ingham is that when compost is properly made, then weed seeds, human pathogens and heavy metals will not be present in detectable levels.

Commercial compost producers and suppliers should have available a report on the levels of the above-listed parameters as well as nutrient levels for each batch of compost they produce. Minimally, when purchasing compost, ensure the compost meets the criteria noted above.

New research by Dr. Graham Lancaster at Southern Cross University in New South Wales, Australia is increasing our understanding of compost. It has been our understanding that compost may not supply all the nutrients necessary for growing turfgrass, and that a standard soil test for the compost would let you know the levels of nutrients. It was thought that compost had lower levels of nutrients when compared to other fertilizers. However, the standard soil chemistry tests for nutrient and mineral content cannot identify the actual quantities in compost because the nutrients are tied up in the organisms and are not detectable by standard extraction methods. The new research shows that the nutrient content of compost can be 100 times greater than previously tested. Dr. Lancaster's work has shown that most agricultural soils have enough nutrients to sustain themselves for hundreds, if not thousands of years with no additional inputs, provided the soil biology is present to make the nutrients available to the plants.

A practical test for compost maturity is to put a handful into a sealed plastic bag and place the bag in a warm room for a week. If the compost smells mushroom-earthy then it's mature. If it stinks, it's not.

Compost is easy to make at home.

Turfgrass Integrated Pest Management (IPM)

WE HAVE BEEN USING CHEMICAL PESTICIDES FOR YEARS TO TRY TO ELIMINATE weeds, insects and diseases from lawns, but these same weeds, insects and diseases keep showing up. You might ask, if the chemicals did what the manufacturers said they did, why do we still have all the pests around? It is both futile and impossible to completely eliminate all pests from our lawns. Instead, it is far better for us and the environment to accept a certain level of pest infestation or damage. The insects, diseases and weeds that are 'problems' in our lawns are natural parts of the environment, and each organism serves a function in that environment. It is only because of our perception that our lawns must be perfect carpets of grass that we have attempted to totally eliminate these pests.

Television and the 'Perfect' Lawn

Where did this perception of the 'perfect' lawn arise? How many of you have watched professional golf tournaments, baseball and football on television, and desired the beautifully maintained, pest-free turfgrass look for your own lawn? But the intense level of maintenance required for these turfgrass applications is not realistic for any home lawn. The turfgrass on TV has been treated with chemical fertilizers and pesticides to attain its artificial look. Your lawn is not the greens, tees and

Our exposure to high-maintenance turf situations such as golf courses has affected our perception of what our home lawns should look like.

fairways at Pine Valley Golf Club in Pine Valley, NJ, or Shinnecock Hills Golf Club in Southampton, NY. You can have a dense, green, organically grown carpet at home, but it just won't be exactly the same as on television.

We are also subjected to mass advertising of products that are designed to help us have the 'perfect' lawn. Ads for weed and feed fertilizers and for pesticides to kill anything that might harm our 'perfect' lawn are ubiquitous during televised sports events, and pervade summer advertising. Do you know that up until the time that scientists discovered a chemical (2,4-D) that would kill broadleaf plants in lawns, clover was an integral member of the lawn community? Yet, when this chemical was discovered, clover and other harmless plants became weeds. How many of you consider clover to be a weed in lawns? How many books and pamphlets have you read that refer to clover as a weed?

Some Good Reasons Not To Use Pesticides*

It is true that we live on a large ball called Earth. If you stop and think about it, when you throw something away, there really is no 'away.' Living, as we do, on the surface of a sphere means we are living in a closed system—what is done in one area affects other areas and affects us all.

The question of whether it is safe to use pesticides is a controversial subject. People on both sides of the question have offered a plethora of reasons why they are right and the other side is wrong. We are left to decide if using pesticides is the right thing to do. At one end of the scale are the companies that produce pesticides, and the related industries that promote, sell and apply pesticides. At the other end of the scale are the people who are concerned with

*see p. 156 for references to endnotes in this section

toxicity of pesticides and what these chemicals are doing by polluting the environment we all share.

This section of the book is not intended to put down pesticides, or to tell you they are bad. The intention of this section is to provide information about pesticides that the pesticide companies would likely not want you to know, or to think about.

According to estimates of pesticide usage in 1994 and 1995, 4.5 billion pounds of pesticides are used annually in the United States.[1] If pesticides worked and truly solved pest problems, we would have far fewer pest problems and would be using a lot less pesticide than we do today.

Applying a pesticide will kill the pests, but it does not change the conditions that encouraged the pests to attack the plants in the first place. Pests, as with all living beings, need certain conditions including air, water, food and shelter, to thrive. Changing the conditions to something more suitable for the plant and less suitable for the pest will reduce or eliminate the pest from the scene. If you know what kinds of pests are likely to attack your lawn, you can plan to reduce or eliminate the conditions that would be inviting to pests before any problems arise.

Unfortunately, pesticides also kill many of the beneficial insects and microorganisms that are necessary for the health of the soil. Pests tend to re-establish their population quicker than the beneficial organisms after a pesticide application, and this leads to a vicious cycle of having to use more pesticides more often.

Pesticides are hazardous to human health. Physician Philip Landrigan of the Mt. Sinai School of Medicine has written, 'the range of these adverse health effects includes acute and persistent injury to the nervous system, lung damage, injury to reproductive organs, dysfunction of the immune and endocrine [hormone] systems, birth defects, and cancer.'[2] It is noted by the Northwest Coalition for Alternatives to Pesticides (NCAP) that on

Killing weeds with herbicide does not change the reason the weeds grew in the first place.

Pesticides can cause acute and chronic problems in humans. Children are especially vulnerable.

'an EPA risk information database that summarizes studies of about 19 of the 28 commonly used pesticides, almost all (18 out of these 19) have caused reproductive problems in laboratory tests, including miscarriages, birth defects, and testicular atrophy.'[3,4]

The Canadian Centre for Occupational Health and Safety has identified acute health effects caused by pesticides in humans. These include nausea; eye, skin, respiratory and throat irritation; muscle spasms; and death.[5]

A 1989 Environment Canada publication notes that repeated exposure to pesticides has been linked to neurological problems, immune system suppression (which creates environmental hypersensitivity), leukemia, brain and lung cancer, Parkinson's disease, kidney damage and non-Hodgkin's lymphoma. It also noted several reproductive disorders,

including endocrine disruption, low sperm count and sterility.[6]

Because pesticides are designed to kill living organisms and a staggering amount of pesticide is used every year, we can expect health-related problems to increase every year, especially if we continue to use pesticides at our current rate.

Children are especially at risk, as their physical bodies are not yet fully developed. Their metabolic systems don't process or excrete toxins the way adults' systems do. They are like little sponges, absorbing all kinds of things during their activities, as well as all the things kids tend to put in their mouths. They spend a lot of time playing on lawns at home, in parks and at school. The more we use pesticides on lawns, the more we expose our children to the effects of those pesticides.

Pets can pick up pesticide residues on their fur and paws.

Pesticides are particularly dangerous for those using them on a regular basis, such as the people who work for lawn-care companies that are involved in pesticide application. They are exposed to the concentrated form of the pesticide and are exposed during application.

Pesticides are hazardous to pets, especially pesticides applied to your lawn. Pets can pick up residues on their fur and paws. Organophosphate pesticides have caused many pet illnesses and deaths.[7] Dogs that were diagnosed with canine malignant lymphoma were more likely than healthy dogs to have come from homes where 2,4-D pesticide was used on the lawn.[8]

Pesticides contaminate water and air. The U.S. Geological Survey's (USGS) national water-quality monitoring program found at least one pesticide in all the samples taken from the major rivers in the U.S. Also shown to be contaminated by at least one pesticide were 99% of urban streams, 92% of streams in agricultural areas, 50% of urban wells and 60% of wells in agricultural areas.[9]

The USGS also made a compilation of air quality studies showing contamination by diazinon (an insecticide) at almost 90%, and chlorpyrifos (an insecticide) at almost 70%, of the samples taken. Two different airborne herbicide contaminants were found in almost 50% (trifluralin) and almost 60% (2,4-D) of all the samples taken. DDT, which was banned over 30 years ago, was still found in 90% of the samples analyzed.[10]

Yes indeed, better living through chemistry! And many people still think there is nothing wrong with applying pesticides. Nothing like a breath of fresh air and a nice clean glass of water.

Pesticides known to cause harm to birds and fish are used in copious amounts every year.[11] There are documented examples of pesticides affecting the environment, such as the flock of Canada Geese that died near Simcoe, Ontario, Canada in September 1996. The autopsies done showed that the grass and clover found in their digestive systems contained diazinon. Diazinon is an organophosphate insecticide that is used on lawns and in agriculture. The geese were reported to have irregular behaviors and showed signs of physical poisoning (blood in the feces and mucus streaming from their mouths).[12] Diazinon is also quite toxic to earthworms, with a 60% mortality rate for populations in lawns sprayed with diazinon.[13] A loss of earthworms severely reduces the nutrient cycling in the soil and increases the incident of thatch build-up. To its credit, the U.S. Environmental Protection Agency has taken steps to phase out all indoor and non-agricultural uses of diazinon.

The sale of pesticides earns a substantial amount of profit for the companies who manufacture them. It is these same companies that sponsor the safety tests of these pesticides. A company that wishes to register a pesticide product has to provide safety data to the regulatory agency to prove its product works and causes no unreasonably adverse effects on the environment. This information is then reviewed by the EPA to see if the product meets the requirements for registration under the Federal Insecticide, Fungicide and Rodenticide Act (FIFRA).[14]

Often, a major portion of the entire list of ingredients in pesticides is hidden by the companies that manufacture those pesticides, under the guise of proprietary information. Pesticides have to have the active ingredient listed on the product label, but often the

Canada geese and other wildlife have been harmed by pesticides.

'inert' ingredients are not listed on the label.[15] Sometimes the 'inert' ingredients are not so inert, but are excluded from most toxicology tests[16] because they are not the active ingredients. The EPA requires that the active ingredients and any inert ingredients on the U.S. Environmental Protection Agency (EPA) List 1 need to be identified and acknowledged. However, there are four lists of inert ingredients listed by the EPA. List 1 contains chemicals known to cause cancer, reproductive toxicity, neurotoxicity, damage to the kidney or liver, or that are acutely toxic to aquatic organisms. List 2 contains potentially toxic inerts that have a high priority for testing. List 3 contains inerts of unknown toxicity, and by far contains the most chemicals of all four lists. List 4 contains substances considered to be of minimal concern. It would be good if these pesticide companies would be forthright in their disclosures about the nature of all the ingredients in their products. It would also be good if those who regulate pesticides would require far greater testing and evaluation of all the ingredients, both alone and mixed together in the various formulations, that comprise pesticide products.

The bottom line is that it is up to us as consumers to ask questions and demand answers from the people who design, manufacture, supply, regulate and apply pesticides, before we blindly accept what they say.

The Northwest Coalition for Alternatives to Pesticides in Eugene, Oregon (www.pesticide.org) and the Sierra Club of Canada (www.sierra-club.ca) are two of many wonderful organizations that are working toward a healthier world. The information contained in this section (including the references and notes) and a ton of other in-depth information about all aspects of pesticides are available from these organizations.

I have been a licenced pesticide applicator and have applied herbicides, fungicides and insecticides. The course I took to qualify for my licence was intense, covering a great many aspects of pesticide use in landscapes and on golf courses. The pesticide applicator course did not, however, present the information that is available through many organizations, including the two listed above. It is important to gather as much information as possible when making any choice. Had I known then what I know now, I would not have chosen to apply pesticides.

The IPM Program

Integrated pest management (IPM) is a program that takes advantage of the natural checks and balances that help keep desirable plants healthy and beautiful. We will never completely eliminate pests and pathogens because they are part of the natural ecosystem. By knowing and understanding the life cycles and habits of pests and pathogens, control programs can be developed that minimize harm and disruptions to the ecosystem. The essence of IPM is to provide the desired quality with minimal ecological, economical and sociological consequences. IPM has also been referred to as 'intelligent plant management' and 'integrated plant management.'

Turfgrass IPM focuses on growing healthy lawns and preventing problems from arising. An IPM program helps you set limits on what level of pest infestation or damage is acceptable in your lawn, and what to do when those limits are reached.

This lawn is showing signs of patchiness and thinning. IPM can help determine the cause of these problems.

Pest attacks in lawns are usually the result of the turfgrass ecosystem being out of balance. Examples of lawn stresses include heavy use and wear, poor management practices and climate conditions (normal or otherwise).

An IPM program for your lawn begins very simply. It evolves over time to encompass all the components of a full IPM program, which has the following requirements:

- managing the landscape (including installation) to prevent any organism from becoming a problem
- monitoring the landscape for organism populations, pest damage and climactic/environmental conditions
- properly identifying pest and beneficial species before any action is taken
- setting threshold limits for injury and action
- using a variety of methods, including cultural, mechanical, physical, biological, behavior modification and chemical to accomplish acceptable control, and using non-damaging, non-polluting methods to deal with problems first before using methods that damage or are toxic to the environment
- evaluating the effectiveness of the program.

Managing the landscape

A healthy lawn begins with healthy soil. Healthy lawns are properly maintained, which means proper mowing, watering and feeding, and following other cultural practices that enhance healthy turfgrass growth. These concepts are outlined in the appropriate sections of this book. A healthy landscape is key to minimizing the conditions needed by pests to establish themselves in the lawn.

Monitoring (scouting) the landscape

The only way to know if pests are attacking your lawn is to monitor, or scout, your lawn on a regular basis. You will then be able to spot the presence and activity of turf pests before any damage can occur. You will have to determine how often you need to scout your lawn. Lawns that are maintained to a higher level, such as a front yard, will need more frequent monitoring than low-maintenance areas, such as a playground or back yard. It is possible to visually inspect a small lawn on a daily basis. Medium-maintenance lawns, no matter the size, should be scouted at least once a week. Low-maintenance lawns can be scouted once every two weeks to once a month. Always monitor for root-feeding insects when they are active, regardless of your monitoring schedule.

As you learn more about turfgrass insects, diseases and weeds, you will know when to monitor for their presence or absence, what symptoms or damage to look for, and what environmental conditions favor their growth.

It is important to keep detailed records of all your observations, including the weather. Many IPM scouts have developed custom data recording sheets to use when they are out monitoring the lawn. You can make your own scouting sheet, but an example is illustrated on page 116. The sheet should include a map of the scouting area to make it easy to record pest hotspots. It is also important to keep detailed records of all your turf maintenance activities, including results of soil tests and soil foodweb assays. This information can be useful in spotting recurring problems and in planning your maintenance regime.

These detailed records will also let you know if any pest-management action you have taken has effectively reduced the pest population to a tolerable level.

Properly identifying pest and beneficial species

It is important to know the identity and life cycles of the members of your turfgrass community. This may seem like a large, daunting task, but each region of our country has only a small number of insect pests, weeds and diseases that cause the most problems. Learn about these pests first, as they are likely the ones you will see. There are multiple sources for information including your local Cooperative Extension, garden centers, horticultural universities, colleges and training facilities, books and the Internet.

You can ask yourself a series of questions to help identify the problem. Is the insect you see a pest species or a beneficial species? Is that an invasive perennial weed that will take over your lawn or an annual weed that will be gone after the next mowing? Is that brown spot a disease, the result of the dog peeing on your lawn, or damage from root-feeding insects? Is the problem you see caused by a pest or by something else in the turfgrass environment? It is only by learning about and properly identifying the members of your lawn ecosystem that you can make sound management decisions.

Insects and weeds are often very easy to identify. Diseases, on the other hand, may be very difficult for the average person to identify. Fortunately there are many public and private pest diagnostic labs that provide this service. Contact your local Cooperative Extension to see if they offer disease identification services. If they do not, they will

Always properly identify insects! This ground beetle is a major predator, and our friend.

know who does. Also make sure that you ask Cooperative Extension or the private lab for directions on how to submit a sample for testing. Your sample should include diseased and non-diseased turf.

Setting threshold limits for injury and action

A healthy lawn can tolerate the presence of pests with no visible damage, but the same level of pests may damage a stressed lawn. It is up to you to determine what levels of pests are acceptable in your lawn, and what levels of pests require you to take action. You may find that you can accept more weeds in your back yard than in your front yard. You may also find that you have a lower tolerance for some pests depending on the amount of damage the pest can do. Setting tolerance and action levels takes much of the guesswork out

of the decision-making process.

Threshold levels have been established for many turfgrass insects, but these levels vary depending on the type of turfgrass grown, the level of management, the current condition of the grass and how much damage you can tolerate. Use these threshold levels as a starting point for your IPM program, making adjustments for your specific conditions (see table on page 118). Thresholds for diseases and weeds have not been established, so you will have to do decide for yourself how much damage or how many weeds you can tolerate.

Management options

Once a problem has been identified and the action threshold has been reached or passed, you must choose a method for control. Cultural controls are the most important. Physical controls should be attempted next, followed by biological controls. Resort to chemical controls only when the first three possibilities have been exhausted.

Cultural controls are the techniques you use in the day-to-day care of your lawn. The best defense against pests and diseases is to maintain a healthy lawn. It is very important to keep your soil healthy, with plenty of organic matter. A healthy soil foodweb is very effective in keeping pest organisms in check. Examples of simple cultural control would be to plant pest-resistant grasses, or to spray your lawn with good-quality compost tea.

Physical controls are generally used to combat insect and mammal problems. An example of physical control would be to erect a fence to keep deer off the lawn. Another example of physical control is popping dandelions out of the lawn with a simple hand tool. Other physical controls include traps, barriers and natural repellents that make plants taste or smell bad to pests.

Biological controls use populations of natural predators. Such organisms that attack turfgrass pests include various beneficial fungi, bacteria, viruses, nematodes and insects. Applying good-quality compost as topdressing or spraying compost tea on your lawn will introduce many of these beneficial species. Other animals such as birds and frogs are also effective at reducing pest populations in your lawn. Encourage these creatures to stay and multiply near your lawn. A birdbath and birdfeeder will encourage birds to feed on a wide variety of insect pests. Many beneficial insects probably already live in your lawn, and you can encourage them by planting appropriate food sources. For example, many beneficial insects eat nectar from flowers such as clover and dandelion.

One form of biological control is the naturally occurring soil bacterium *Bacillus thuringiensis* var. *kurstaki,* or *B.t.* for short. It breaks down the gut lining of some insect pests and is available in garden centers. However, *B.t.* can harm or kill many beneficial insects in your lawn, so large applications of it are not a good idea. Very small, targeted applications of very minute amounts may be acceptable.

Chemical controls (pesticides) can be either organic or synthetic and should be used only as a last resort because they can harm the beneficial insects as well as the pests. Another drawback is that they tend to strip away the protective coating of bacteria and fungi that live on the plant surface. Once this layer has been removed, the plant is vulnerable to attack by pest organisms. But if you have tried cultural, physical and biological methods and still wish to take further action, obtain a list of pesticides recommended for that particular disease or insect. Try to use 'organic' types of pesticides that do not harm the environment, are less toxic and are more precisely targeted; they are available at most garden centers. Organic sprays are no less dangerous than chemical ones, but they will break down into harmless compounds, often much sooner than synthetic compounds. Always choose the least toxic option that has the shortest residual activity.

When using pesticides, follow the manufacturer's instructions carefully. NEVER overuse any pesticide. A large amount of pesticide—organic or not— is no more effective in controlling pests than the recommended amount. Also

Backyards and out-of-the-way areas often have higher pest thresholds than showcase front lawns.

note that if a particular pest is not listed on the package, it will not be controlled by that product. Any treatment you choose should be applied when the pest is most vulnerable to the treatment and only when the action threshold has been reached. Only spray the infected area (spot spray), rather than applying blanket coverage.

It is my belief that any pesticide we apply disrupts the balance of microorganisms in the soil profile, kills many beneficial insects and sets us on the vicious circle of having to use those products to control their problems. I would like to see all forms of pesticides eliminated, or at least severely reduced, with people willing to accept some pest damage. Remember, a healthy lawn with a healthy soil foodweb is very effective at resisting pests.

Evaluating the effectiveness of the program

The important final step in your IPM program is to evaluate how effectively your turf-management and pest-control practices are working. Your detailed records of all your lawn-maintenance activities can be compared to previous years' records to answer questions and help you make

Your home lawn IPM program can easily expand to include your whole landscape.

sound management decisions for next year. Are your management practices keeping your lawn healthy, with pests well below tolerable levels? If you had to take action, was the pest population reduced enough to prevent excessive damage, and is it likely that the problem will reoccur? Were the controls you implemented cost-effective? Do you need to modify any control measures to make them more effective? Is it possible to raise the damage and action threshold levels as the lawn becomes healthier? A thorough evaluation will help you adjust your IPM program and help it develop over time.

Starting Your Own Home IPM Program

Now that you have been introduced to the basics of IPM, it's time to implement your IPM program for your lawn. It is a good idea to write down your intentions for implementing an IPM program. A simple statement might be 'I intend to reduce and eliminate the use of pesticides and chemical fertilizers on my lawn.' Some people will set a goal for accomplishing their intentions by a certain date, which can provide a good basis to measure your progress. You can also note your statement of intent on your scouting records as a reminder of why you are doing the IPM in the first place.

Site assessment

When beginning an IPM program, the first step is to do a site assessment. Begin by making a map of your lawn areas. An overhead site map of your property makes the job easy. A simple drawing that is roughly to scale will suffice for the task. Make copies of this map for future scouting use. You can have separate maps for each turf area if you have a large property.

Once you have a map, gather information about your site. Include as much of the following information as possible:
- the type of soil on your property and if the soil type is the same for all turfgrass areas (include all the results of your soil tests and foodweb assays)

- the species of turfgrass in your lawn and the depth of the roots
- the drainage patterns and location of drainage tile, if installed
- the irrigation system, if installed, including the location of the sprinkler heads and their state of operation
- any elevation change such as a slope or depression
- the shaded areas of your lawn, with seasonal variations included
- the lawn traffic patterns
- landscape areas such as planting beds, patios, sidewalks and water features
- all current and historical information about maintenance practices
- any historical information of past pest problems, when those problems happened and what action was taken
- any other problem area that is not pest related.

The site assessment may seem like a lot of work, and it is, but the more information you can gather, the easier your future IPM tasks will be.

During your initial site assessment, make note of any insects, weeds or diseased lawn areas you see, and begin to develop pest profiles for these organisms. Develop pest profiles for the major insects, weeds and diseases that may affect the lawn in your geographical area. Now is also the time to designate the level of maintenance you intend to perform for each area of your lawn. Are some areas high maintenance and some areas low maintenance? This designation will help you set your threshold levels for pests for each area.

There is much information available to help you develop your pest profiles. Each pest profile should contain as much information about that pest as possible, including:

- the common and scientific name of the pest
- damage symptoms to look for when the pest is active
- the seasonal and environmental conditions that favor pest development and activity
- the biology of the pest, including its life cycle, identifying features, timing and mode of action of damage, where the pest can be found and the stages in the pest's life cycle that are susceptible to controls
- scouting techniques for different situations, including predictive models, such as the expected timing of a certain insect appearance or certain plant blooming
- threshold levels for the level or levels of turf maintenance you have selected
- cultural control methods; include the conditions that favor the pest and the maintenance practices that make the turfgrass less favorable for the pest
- physical control methods; not every turfgrass pest has a physical control
- biological control methods; include any available products and the products' attributes
- chemical control methods; always list the least toxic option first.

Once you have created your pest profiles, obtain a year-at-a-glance calendar. Using colored pens or pencils, shade the dates on the calendar to indicate when each pest should be monitored. A calendar like this will help you keep track of what you should be scouting for, and when you should be scouting for it. It makes no sense to scout for a pest that is not likely to be present when you are scouting. (See p. 123.)

IPM Scouting Form for Home Lawns

Date:	Height of lawn:
Location: (front yard, back yard, etc.)	Last mowing date:
Weather conditions:	Soil moisture level:

Insects				Diseases				Weeds				Other Problems			
scouting method used:				% disease coverage:				% weed coverage:				damage seen:			
damage seen:				scouting method used:				scouting method used:							
	Insect present	Threshold reached	Action taken		Disease present	Threshold reached	Action taken		Weed present	Threshold reached	Action taken		Problem present	Threshold reached	Action taken
June Beetle	❏	❏	❏	Pink Snow Mold	❏	❏	❏	Dandelion	❏	❏	❏	Chemical Spill	❏	❏	❏
Japanese Beetle	❏	❏	❏	Fusarium Patch	❏	❏	❏	Canada Thistle	❏	❏	❏	Compaction	❏	❏	❏
European Chafer	❏	❏	❏	Coprinus Snow Mold	❏	❏	❏	Creeping Harebell	❏	❏	❏	Dog Urine	❏	❏	❏
Black Turfgrass Ataenius	❏	❏	❏	Dollar Spot	❏	❏	❏	Ground Ivy	❏	❏	❏	Poor Maintenance	❏	❏	❏
Craneflies: Larvae	❏	❏	❏	Fairy Ring	❏	❏	❏	Crabgrass	❏	❏	❏	Thatch	❏	❏	❏
Billbug: Adult	❏	❏	❏	Leaf Spot and Melting Out	❏	❏	❏	Quackgrass	❏	❏	❏	Turf Wear	❏	❏	❏
Billbug: Larvae	❏	❏	❏	Powdery Mildew	❏	❏	❏	Other	❏	❏	❏	Winterkill	❏	❏	❏
Chinch Bug	❏	❏	❏	Pythium Blight	❏	❏	❏					Other	❏	❏	❏
Cutworm	❏	❏	❏	Pythium Root Rot	❏	❏	❏	**Site Map**							
Armyworm	❏	❏	❏	Red Thread	❏	❏	❏								
Sod Webworm	❏	❏	❏	Rhizoctonia Blight	❏	❏	❏								
Other	❏	❏	❏	Snow Scald	❏	❏	❏								
Notes				Summer Patch	❏	❏	❏								
				Typhula Blight	❏	❏	❏								
				Other	❏	❏	❏								

Scouting tips and tools

For a home lawn, the monitoring technique most often used is walking around for a visual observation. Some tools will make the task of IPM scouting much easier.

- a 10x to 20x hand lens is great for identifying turf insects as well as disease symptoms and lesions. Proper identification is extremely important. A misidentification could result in unnecessary actions being taken.
- use a clipboard and pencil to record your observations on the scout data recording forms you constructed earlier. Pencils are good because they work when it's wet and when it's cold.
- a pocket knife with a 3–4" blade
- small vials for collecting insects. A good option is to use empty film containers (for those of you who still take pictures with film), which are available in quantity from places that develop pictures.
- Ziplock baggies for turfgrass and weed samples. You will need a way to identify the samples once they have been collected. Masking tape works great to note the location and date you took the sample.
- a coffee can with both ends removed for insect scouting
- a 1-gallon container for mixing a soap solution; mild dishwashing detergent
- a sharp spade that can make nice clean, straight cuts can be used to check the rootzone under the turf.
- if you are taking samples of weeds or disease it is a good idea to have a cooler to keep the samples fresh, especially in hot weather when samples can degrade quickly.
- a square waterproof frame, 1–2' per side, for use with soap flushing and visual observation. The frame is used for sampling random spots on your lawn. After sampling a spot, pick up the frame, walk a few steps and place the frame on the ground.

Scouting for Insects

Some insect pests can be scouted using straight visual observation. Methods are available to aid in visual scouting, such as soap flushes, tin cans and pitfall traps. Many scouting methods involve spending some time on your knees. If your lawn appears healthy, the location of your sampling spots can be random. If you notice damage, sample a few spots at the edge of the damaged area.

White grubs can be monitored by examining several areas of soil underneath the grass, particularly at the edges of problem areas. Use a spade to cut three sides of a 1' square of grass. Cut down to expose at least 2" of soil. Fold the grass back carefully, using the uncut edge as a hinge. Remove the dirt, and count the number of exposed grubs. Look also to see if the roots have been damaged. Then fold the grass back into place, tamp it and water it. In well-managed, healthy lawns, up to 15 grubs per square foot can be present without causing any appreciable damage to the turf. In stressed or poorly managed lawns, however, 15 grubs per square foot might seriously damage the grass. Make note of any other larvae or insects you discover.

Include your children when you are out scouting your lawn. It can be educational and entertaining for them and for you, and kids love bugs (even though some say they don't).

Soap flush for monitoring turf insects

Mix 1–2 tablespoons of liquid dish soap (not detergent) in a gallon of water. Do not use more soap than recommended. Concentrated soap solutions can burn the turfgrass blades. Soap flushes irritate the insects, forcing them to the surface for relatively easy counting. Soap flushes are useful for monitoring active insects and larvae, such as craneflies (leatherjackets), sod webworms, other moth and butterfly larval pest, and chinch bugs.

There are a couple of ways to use a soap flush. One method is to place your waterproof frame on the lawn and soak the area with the soap solution. Use a watering can to slowly soak the area, thus helping to avoid runoff from the test area. Make sure the top couple of inches of soil are soaked. Observe the area closely for 10–15 minutes and see what comes to the surface. Count and remove the pests you spot. Caterpillars and leatherjackets can be picked off by hand. A wet/dry vacuum works well for removing pests. The other soap flush method is the tin can method. Remove both ends from a large tin can—a coffee can works well. Push one end of the can a couple of inches into the soil. Pour the soapy solution into the top of the can and see what floats up after a few minutes. For chinch bugs, you can fill the tin can with plain water. Sample at least 10 spots for small yards, and more for larger yards.

Sample insect threshold levels

Use the following threshold levels as a starting point for your IPM program. For example, if you see eight June Beetle white grubs in a sample and the turf is relatively healthy, you can adjust your threshold level up. The threshold levels given here are for an irrigated lawn. Lawns without irrigation will have a lower threshold.

Pest	Number of insects per square foot	Pest	Number of insects per square foot
White grubs: June Beetle	3–5	Craneflies: Larvae	3–5
White grubs: Japanese Beetle	3–5	Billbugs: Adult	1
		Billbugs: Larvae	20-25
White grubs: European Chafer	3–5	Chinch Bugs	25–35
		Cutworms	1
White grubs: Black turfgrass ataenius	5–8	Armyworms	1
		Sod Webworms	3–8

If you are using the tin can method, you will have to adjust your threshold levels to reflect the size of the area sampled. The formula for the area of a circle is $A = \pi r2$ (3.14 times the radius times the radius). If your tin can has a diameter of 6" then the radius is 3", thus the area your can samples is 3.14 x 3" x 3" = 28.25 square inches or about 0.2 square feet. If your threshold level for chinch bugs is 35 insects per square foot, the threshold level for your tin can would be 35 insects per square foot x 0.2 square feet = 7 chinch bugs per tin can sample.

Plant growth and scouting for insects

Insects, like plants, require a specific temperature to begin their growth. As the seasons change from winter to spring and the temperature rises above a critical point, plants and insects awake from their winter slumber. Observe the trees, shrubs and other common plants in your area and their stage of growth. Turfgrass entomologists (entomology is the study of insects) use the annual growth cycles of these common plants to indicate when insect activity is likely to be observed. As you are scouting, note the stage of growth of the local plants and what insect activity you are observing. You do not have to be a plant expert to note that your neighbor's yellow-flowered shrub in the southeast part of his front yard is in full bloom and a certain insect activity was observed. Know also that insect problems will occur at about the same time every year. Recording this information will help you fine-tune your scouting skills for future years.

The Pest Profiles

THE FOLLOWING SAMPLE PEST profiles (one each for insects, weeds and diseases) contain a lot of information for each pest, and as with the site assessment, it may seem like a lot of work to gather so much information. But you only need to gather the information about each pest once. It is possible to get by with less information than is shown in the sample, but the more information you have on each pest, the easier it will be to form a plan of action to monitor and deal with each pest. It is always good policy to research new, non-toxic, environmentally friendly ways of dealing with pests.

The information presented in each pest profile is not difficult to gather, especially if you use a computer and an Internet search engine such as google.com or dogpile.com. For example, to look up information on sod webworm, type in either the name 'sod webworm' or '*Parapediasia teterrella*.' You can mix and match those names with terms like life cycle, identification, damage, IPM, control, etc. The information can also be found in books from your local library, from local nurseries and garden centers, Cooperative Extension, and from local agricultural or horticultural colleges and universities.

Sample insect pest profile

June Beetle
Phyllophaga spp.

Symptoms

Localized patches of pale, discolored and dying turf displaying symptoms of moisture stress. Damaged areas are small at first, but increase in size as larvae (white grubs) grow and expand their feeding territory. Turf in such areas will have a spongy feel underfoot, and the turf can easily be lifted from the soil surface or rolled up like a carpet.

Favorable environmental conditions

White grubs prefer light and acid soils. Inadequate irrigation and drought stress may compound the damage.

Life cycle

The life cycle of June beetles takes three years to complete. Adult beetles emerge from the soil in early May. The adults are only active at night, flying to find suitable deciduous trees and shrubs to feed on. Females lay eggs in late May and June, ⅛–⅜" deep in the soil. In 2–3 weeks the eggs hatch and the young larvae begin to feed on roots and underground plant parts until early fall (length of larvae is ½"). When the soil warms in spring the larvae continue feeding on roots and underground plant parts. In early fall they burrow into the soil below the frost line to overwinter. In the third summer the larvae pupate in earthen cells in the soil. The subsequent adults remain inactive, ⅝–¾" below the soil line, until the following May.

ID

June beetles are large, robust beetles, ¾–1" in length. They are brown to brownish black with prominent, club-like antenna. The eggs are pearly white, approximately ⅛" x ¹⁄₁₆". The larvae (white grubs) are white and crescent or C-shaped with a hard brown head and a fleshy, legless abdomen. Mature larvae are 1–1⅝" in length. Pupae are oval shaped and brownish. The larvae of June beetles can be distinguished from other white grubs by the patterns of their anal slits and rasters.

Life cycle stages susceptible to management

The larval stage is most susceptible to control measures.

Scouting/monitoring

Larvae: Sampling should begin early in the predicted activity period and before signs of damage are present. Because distribution is not uniform, samples should be taken in a consistent, uniform pattern. Enough samples should be taken to ensure reasonably accurate coverage of the area. For home lawns, spacing of about 10' between sampling sites, or 4 casual paces for most people, is adequate. For large lawns, increase the distance between sample sites.

You will need to examine the underside of the turfgrass to count larvae populations. Deep irrigation the day before monitoring will bring the larvae closer to the soil surface. Cut 1 ft² of sod on three sides with a spade and peel it back to expose the underside of the turf. Examine the top 2" of the rootzone for the presence of grubs and note the number found. Replace the sod and water it right away.

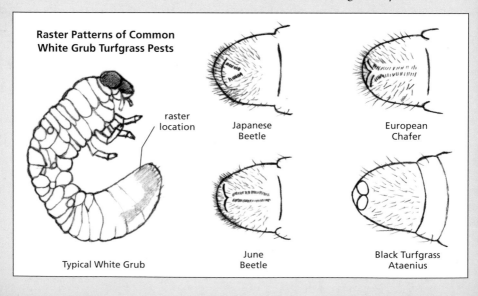

Raster Patterns of Common White Grub Turfgrass Pests

raster location

Japanese Beetle

European Chafer

Typical White Grub

June Beetle

Black Turfgrass Ataenius

Adult: Adults eat the leaves and flowers of many deciduous trees and shrubs, and can be a nuisance in buildings and around lights during their flight period. Monitoring for adults will only show they are present, not how many there are or where their eggs have been laid. Monitoring can be accomplished with a light trap. Note the number of adults trapped over the flight period.

Threshold levels

A population average of 3–5 larvae per square foot is a good threshold level to begin your program. If your lawn is healthy at this level then no treatment is required. You may need to take action if the population rises above this number. The threshold can be adjusted depending on whether the area is a showcase front lawn or a lawn used as groundcover between a garage and an alley.

Cultural controls

Maintaining your turf for optimal health is an important preventative measure.

Biological controls

Birds, predatory insects, moles, skunks, predatory nematodes, parasitic wasps and flies, and bacterial and fungal pathogens attack June beetles and their larvae. There is also a product that, by mimicking the insect-molting hormone, causes premature molting and death of the insect.

Chemical controls

For chemical control to be most effective, mow your lawn short and irrigate deeply to bring the grubs closer to the surface. The first week of August is the prime time for grub control as most of the eggs have hatched, and the small grubs are feeding close to the surface. However, some eggs are laid in late July, and these will hatch by the third week in August. Heavy feeding begins in September.

- Treat when the larvae are young and are most susceptible to biological and chemical products.
- Treat when the larvae are close to the surface, so that a drench with a liquid product can physically be in contact with the grubs and have an effect on them.
- Spring treatments are a waste of pesticide and money, as they won't affect fall populations.

Evaluation procedure

The evaluation process should be done for every pest you have identified and noted as part of your IPM program for your lawn. The questions listed below can be adjusted for each insect pest profile.

- Was the monitoring program effective?
- Does the frequency of monitoring need to increase, or can it be decreased?
- Were there any instances of the insect larvae or adults seen during the monitoring period? If there were, was there enough damage to exceed your action threshold?
- Do you need to adjust your threshold level?
- Were your maintenance practices and control procedures effective, and do they need to be adjusted?
- Is there any new information, processes or products that could be of benefit to control this insect?
- Is there less damage this year than previous years?
- Are there fewer adults being trapped in the light traps?

Notes on some other insects to get you started on your pest profiles

Japanese beetle
Popillia japonica

There is one generation of Japanese beetle per year. The adults are stout, ½" long, and metallic green and bronze in color. The adults emerge in early July and begin feeding on a wide range of trees and shrubs for about 1–1½ months. After mating, the female beetles lay 1–4 eggs at a depth of 1–2" in the soil under the turfgrass. One female can lay 60 eggs in her lifetime. Larvae hatch in about two weeks and begin feeding on the roots in the upper 4" of soil. The grubs mature by late summer to early fall, reaching a length of ¾", and are usually found near the soil surface. As winter approaches and the soil cools, the grubs dig deeper into the soil (below the frost level) to overwinter. As the soil warms in spring, the grubs return to the surface to feed, usually in April or May. If you notice adults on your trees and shrubs, you will likely have the grubs in your lawn.

European chafer
Rhizotrogus majalis

There is one generation of European chafer per year. European chafer adults closely resemble June beetles, but they are smaller and a lighter tan color.

Japanese beetles

European chafer adults emerge from the lawn in mid-June to mid-July. The adults swarm to nearby trees at sundown to mate. European chafers feed very little on trees and shrubs. Their emergence from the soil is mostly for mating. The females return to the nearby lawns and lay their eggs in the soil. The eggs hatch in about two weeks, and the young grubs feed near the surface. Lack of moisture can delay the eggs hatching. During periods of summer drought, grubs may remain deep in the soil where moisture is available. The grubs reach their mature size by the end of September, and can cause a lot of damage at that time. As the cold weather approaches, the grubs dig themselves deeper into the soil. The grubs migrate closer to the surface as the soil warms in spring. Feeding ends by late May, and the grubs enter their pupal stage. If you notice the mating flight in June or early July, you are likely to have some turf damage by fall.

Black turfgrass ataenius
Ataenius spretulus

There are two generations of Black turfgrass ataenius each year. The adults are dark brown to black, approximately ¼" long. The adults overwinter in loose soil, pine needles and leaf litter, and they begin moving into turfgrass in March or April. Females deposit eggs into soil and thatch. After the eggs hatch, the larvae (white grubs) feed on grass roots for 3–5 weeks before pupating. First-generation adults emerge around mid-July. Eggs are laid and the second generation of larvae begins appearing in late July or early August, maturing into overwintering adults by October. Black turfgrass ataenius larvae are almost identical to other species of white grubs but are much smaller.

Sample White Grub Life Cycles and Scouting Times

	Jan	Feb	Mar	Apr	May	Jun	Jul	Aug	Sep	Oct	Nov	Dec
June Beetle												
Japanese Beetle												
European Chafer												
Black Turfgrass Ataenius												

	egg
	larva
	pupa
	adult
	scouting

The June beetle, Japanese beetle, European chafer and black turfgrass ataenius all have white grubs as larvae, and control techniques are similar. The grubs can be distinguished from each other by the pattern of spines (known as rasters) on the tip of their abdomens (see p. 120). Skunks and birds can damage lawns in spring and fall when the white grubs are growing and feeding near the soil surface. Flocks of birds feeding on your lawn is a sign that you should check for grub infestations.

Sod webworm
Parapediasia teterrella

Sod webworms are the larvae of small, brownish white 'snout moths.' Adults are ½–¹¹⁄₁₆" long with a wingspan of ⅝–¾". The wings fold around the body at rest to give a cylindrical appearance. The wings and the body may be covered with colorful, iridescent scales. The palps (scaly mouthparts) of the adult are often long and project forward into a snout. Larvae are creamy white to dark gray with light brown heads, and bodies up to ¾" long that may have dark spots and possibly a few short hairs.

Adults are active in July, August and September. They fly at night in erratic flight patterns over the grass, dropping eggs as they fly, or placing the eggs at the base of the grass plants. Adults spend the day hiding in the grass, on tree trunks or in shrubs. Eggs hatch in about a week and larvae begin night feeding on the nearby grass plants. The larvae construct silken cases in the thatch or soil, where they take their cut-off grass blades to eat. The larvae overwinter in the silken cases and resume activity the following spring. After feeding for a short time, they spin gray, silken cocoons (just below soil level) to pupate in early summer. Moths are noticed all summer because of overlapping generations.

Armyworm and fall armyworm
Pseudaletia unipuncta and *Spodoptera frugiperda*

Armyworms and fall armyworms are mostly agricultural pests of cereal crops that also feed on turfgrass. They are larvae of night-flying moths in the Noctuidae family. Adults are fat-bodied, generally dull brown to tan to gray, with a wing span of up to 1½". The fore wings are mottled brown and gray, while the hind wings are shiny silver-white with a dark, narrow edge. Larvae are hairless and range in color from yellow-green to dark brown to gray. Mature armyworm larvae can reach up to 2" in length. Young larvae are as small as ¹⁄₁₆" long. The larvae have three stripes running the length of their body, one on top and one on each side. Fall armyworm larvae have the stripes and a yellow-white Y-marking on the head and four dark circular spots on the upper side of each abdominal segment.

Armyworms overwinter as larvae in the soil or under debris. The larvae continue to eat and grow except during very cold weather. Mature larvae pupate in silk cocoons in the soil or under leaf litter. Adults first emerge in May and June. Mating takes place at night. Adult females feed for about 7 days before laying clusters of up to 130 eggs on your lawn. A single female can lay up to 2000 eggs in her lifetime. The young larvae immediately begin feeding on leaves at night or during cloudy weather, and then often hide in the thatch during the day. Damage appears as roughly round patches of defoliated turf. It takes about a month from when the eggs hatch for the larvae to reach mature size. Armyworms may have as many as three generations per growing season. Armyworms do not overwinter in the northern US, but migrate north during the growing season. Armyworms often group themselves together and move en masse to new food sources, causing lawn and plant damage along the way.

Billbug
Sphenophorus spp.

There are a couple of different species of billbugs that attack turfgrass. Billbugs are members of the weevil family and have the characteristic weevil beak-like snouts. Adults are dark gray, black, brown or reddish brown, and are often covered in soil. They range in length from ¼–½", depending on the species. The larvae are creamy white and legless, ¼–½" long, with brown heads.

Billbugs have one-year life cycles. Adults overwinter in thick thatch and under leaf litter, and become active in spring when the soil temperature rises above 50° F. After feeding for a short time, the adults disperse and begin egg-laying in May and June. The adult female chews a small hole in the grass stem or leaf sheath and deposits an egg

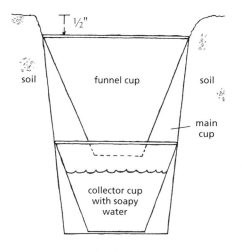

PitFall Trap

in the hole. The females prefer laying their eggs near areas that warm up quickly in spring, such as sidewalks and patios, or anyplace in full sun. After the eggs hatch, the young larvae begin feeding inside the stem or leaf sheath, which causes fine, sawdust-like matter to accumulate inside the stem or leaf sheath. This injury causes leaf browning and death. A handful of damaged grass is easy to pull up, as the leaf stalks break easily. This sawdust-like matter is also present near the turfgrass crowns when the growing larvae exit the plant and enters the soil. Older larvae feed on plant roots. Damage appears as small dead patches that can be confused with damage from other pests or from drought. Heavy infestation can kill an entire lawn. Larvae mature in 1–2 months, and pupate in the soil under the thatch. The new adults emerge in 8 to 10 days.

Scout for billbugs on sunny days. Observe sidewalks, driveways, patios and similar areas near your lawn for the presence of adults. Adults rarely fly but usually walk from lawn to lawn, letting you know that billbugs are in the area. A pitfall trap can be used for more accurate samples, and is best used when the adults are active in spring. Place small plastic cups in holes cut in random spots in the lawn (save the turf plug and keep it watered). If using the pitfall trap method for sampling billbugs, begin with a threshold level of 2–4 adults per cup per day.

Chinch bug
Blissus leucopterus
Chinch bugs have piercing mouth parts and suck the juices out of the crown and stems of turfgrass plants. They also inject salivary fluid into the plant, which disrupts the water flow in the plant, causing wilt and often death. A couple of species are pests, but the most common chinch bug in the northern US is the hairy chinch bug (*Blissus leucopterus hirtus*). Young nymphs are bright red; as the nymphs age they become a darker brick red to gray-brown with a white band across the abdomen. Adults, which are $\frac{3}{16}$–$\frac{1}{4}$" in length, have white forewings and a triangular black spot between the wings.

Chinch bugs have a one-year life cycle. Adult chinch bugs overwinter in groups in leaf litter and debris under trees and shrubs, and move out into the lawn in spring (May and June) as the temperature warms. Egg-laying begins as the adults become active. Young chinch bug nymphs appear as early as late May, and mature into adults by mid-summer. Minor damage is not often observed until the middle of July, and heavy damage can be seen by August, especially if the weather has been hot and dry. Damage is seen as irregular, sunken, yellow to brown patches. Chinch bugs tend to hang around in groups, and damage is often localized. Chinch bugs smell bad when crushed, and the odor can let you know that chinch bugs are present. The odor may be especially noticeable after the lawn is mowed. You will need to scout for chinch bugs throughout the growing season.

Scouting for Weeds
Weeds are truly just plants growing where you don't want them to grow, and likely there is a seed bank already in your lawn. Poor maintenance practices, poor environmental conditions for turfgrass, an unbalanced soil food-web, and damage from insects, disease and other agents open up space for weeds to invade.

This lawn has 60%+ weeds, and is a candidate for lawn re-establishment.

Scouting for weeds is easy. Small yards can be visually inspected, and an estimate made of the percentage of weeds present. Use the transect method for large yards:

- Take a large step onto your lawn and look at the area around your front foot. Is there a weed there?
- Proceed in a straight line across the lawn, stopping every 5–10 paces to look for the presence of weeds.
- Turn around and make another pass across the lawn in the same fashion. You can walk in parallel lines or a zigzag pattern.
- Count the number of stops you make and the number of times you saw weeds when you stopped.
- The number of weed instances divided by the number of stops times 100 will give you a rough percentage

of weed cover. If you make 5 passes and stop 10 times per pass that equals 50 stops. If you spotted weeds at 10 of those stops, then you have about 20% weed coverage.

Weed thresholds

How many weeds can you accept in your lawn? Generally, if your lawn has a 5–10% weed population then nothing needs to be done. If the weed population is higher than 10%, take steps to reduce the population. It has been suggested that if your lawn has 50% or more weeds then it is time for lawn re-establishment.

Weed control

The lawn may contain a high population of unwanted grasses, grasses that are not adapted to your region or broad-leaved weeds. You will want to remove as many weeds as possible. Broad-leaved weeds can be dug out, removing as much of the root systems as possible. Grassy weeds, such as quack grass, are not the easiest plants to remove from a lawn. Small, isolated patches can be dug out and either seeded or sodded.

The organic method is to pull weeds as you see them. Sometimes, with weeds such as dandelions, part of the root will break off and the part left in the ground will regenerate the top growth. Successive removal of the regenerated top growth will eventually deplete the root of energy, and the weed dies.

The best time to remove weeds is when they are young and have not developed an extensive root system. Pull most weeds, such as dandelions, by hand. Try and get as much root out as possible. For tough perennial weeds such as Canada thistle, which has an impressive and large root system, the least toxic method is to gradually starve the plants to death. Remove the tops of these weeds as close to the ground as possible. Continue to remove all the new growth as it appears until you eventually deplete the root system of any stored energy. If you have not been able to pull out dandelion-like weeds, at minimum remove all the flowers to reduce the amount of seeds going into your lawn.

Some weeds are good indicators of problems in the lawn.
- The presence of clover that was not intentionally seeded there is an indicator of low fertility.
- Creeping Charlie (ground ivy) grows well in shaded lawns with poor drainage.
- Crabgrass and annual bluegrass often become pests in lawns that are mowed too short and overwatered.

If your lawn has a good population of a variety of weeds, it is possible that the soil is poor (unbalanced foodweb, nutrient availability, pH, drainage, compaction), or that your maintenance practices need adjustment. It is always good to note the conditions in which the weeds are growing as you do your scouting.

If you choose to use chemical weed killers, spot spray only. Do not spray your entire lawn—it does not need it! Always follow the instructions on the label of any weed, insect or disease control product. Avoid weed and feed products. These spread pesticide over your entire lawn, which often does not require any pesticide, and at rates much higher than if you were to just spray a herbicide for weed control. Weed and feed products are not the magic bullet of lawn maintenance.

Lawn approaching 50% weed coverage

Corn gluten meal, which has been shown to be an effective pre-emergent herbicide, can help prevent weed seeds from germinating in the spring.

It is important to note here that a soil foodweb that has more bacterial biomass than fungal mass will favor weeds over the perennial turfgrass species we want to grow. A 1:1 bacterial to fungal biomass ratio is ideal for turfgrass.

Sample weed pest profile
Dandelion
Taraxacum officinale

ID
Dandelion leaves are simple and variously lobed, ¼–¾" long, and have a basal arrangement. The yellow flower heads grow ¾–1½" across. The outer bracts (modified leaves that appear just under the flower) are reflexed (bent downwards). The flowers are borne on long, hollow, leafless stems up to 20" tall. The leaves and the stems contain a milky juice. Dandelions are in the Asteraceae family.

Some weeds, including dandelions, will adapt to the height you mow your lawn. They will send up flowers that bloom at just below your height of cut.

Lifecycle and reproduction methods

Dandelions are simple perennials that reproduce by seed and have a long taproot. Dandelions produce seeds apomicticly (without fertilization), with the seeds pale gray to olive, ³⁄₃₂" long, and having a pappus (the umbrella-like bit that helps the seeds disperse through the air). Traffic, water and especially wind can spread the seeds. The dandelion will regenerate from its taproot if enough of it remains in the soil after physical removal of the plant.

Where the weed is found

Dandelions prefer clay soils but are generally not fussy about where they live. Soils with excess potassium are more prone to dandelion infestation.

Life cycle stages susceptible to management

The most susceptible stage of growth is the young rosette stage, before flowering.

Scouting/monitoring

Look for dandelion rosettes or flowers.

Threshold levels

Depends on scouting method used. The visual scan method is the most often used method. For larger lawns or lawns with an odd shape, it may be better to use the transect method. Weed thresholds are often set by percentage of coverage when using the visual scanning method. A dandelion population of 20% is often high enough for people to take action.

Cultural controls

Physical removal is an effective method. There are a number of dandelion-removal products available and it is important to find one that you feel comfortable using. I prefer a simple dandelion popper. Attempt to remove as much of the taproot as possible. The more you can remove, the less energy reserves the root will have to regenerate a new plant. Physical removal is easiest when the soil is moist. When plant removal is not possible, at least remove the flowers before they go to seed.

Other methods include sizzweeding (flame weeding), the use of flame heat to damage the weed enough to kill it. This technique uses a propane-powered torch, sometimes called a tiger torch, to pass a hot flame over the weed. The flame damages the plant cells by heating the sap and bursting the cell walls. Wilting and death occur within hours. Hold the flame 4–6" over the weed for a few seconds only. Burning all the top growth to a crisp is not an effective use of this technology because the majority of the root system remains to regenerate a new plant.

Note that sizzweeding, as well as spraying vinegar and using boiling water (see below), will damage all the plants surrounding the weed, and some minor repair work may be needed.

Biological controls
Studies are being done to find diseases and insects that will control dandelions. As of this writing, no products are available.

Chemical controls
Corn gluten meal is a pre-emergent weed control product. It prevents seeds from germinating but doesn't harm already living plants. Vinegar kills many plants, including turfgrass and dandelions. Spray it directly onto weed to cover the leaf surface. It is not necessary to soak the weed. Water is technically a chemical, and pouring boiling water on a dandelion will effectively kill it. A blast of super-heated steam has the same effect as sizzweeding.

Evaluation process
Weeds are probably the easiest pests to monitor for, and to evaluate the effectiveness of the program.
- Was the monitoring program effective?
- Does the frequency of monitoring need to increase, or can it be decreased?
- Were there any instances of the weed seen during the year?
- If there was, was there enough damage to exceed your action threshold?
- Do you need to adjust your threshold level?
- Were your maintenance practices and control procedures effective, and do they need to be adjusted?
- Is there any new information, processes or products that could be of benefit in controlling this weed?

Notes on some other weeds to get you started on your pest profiles
See appendix 'Common Turfgrass Weeds,' p. 153, for a list of other common weeds.

Plantain
Plantago major
Plantain is a simple perennial that spreads by seeds. It has a short, thick rootstock anchored by tough, fibrous roots. Plantain has broad leaves, 4–12" in length, oval to ovate in shape, with 5–7 ribs, and smooth or hairy in texture. The margins are smooth or somewhat toothed. The flowers are small and inconspicuous, greenish, and grouped on narrow spikes. The stems are up to 2' tall, leafless, with the flower spike on top. Plantain is a prolific producer of seeds, which are in egg-shaped capsules about 1/32" long, angular, variable in shape, marked with fine, wavy ridges, dark brown and sticky. Plantain prefers well-drained soils, but will grow almost anywhere.

Black medic
Medicago lupulina
Black medic is an annual that has a taproot and reproduces by seed. The compound leaves are alternately arranged on the stem. The leaflets are narrow to broadly obovate (like an

Black medic

upside-down egg), wedge shaped at the base, and have toothed margins. The flowers are small, yellow and irregular, and are borne on a short spike-like flower cluster called a raceme. The stems are prostrate, 8–32" long, and branched at the base. The seedpods are ridged, kidney shaped, contain one seed and are black at maturity. Black medic prefers dry, coarse soils with a high pH.

Canada thistle
Cirsium arvense
Canada thistle is a creeping perennial that reproduces by seeds and rhizomes. Leaves are alternately arranged on the stem, lance shaped, irregularly lobed, spiny toothed with crinkled margins, a smooth upper leaf surface and a usually hairy leaf underside. The stems can be up to 5' tall, branching only at the top, with no hair and very leafy. The flowers are lavender disc flowers borne on numerous heads, ¾" or less in diameter, surrounded by bracts without spiny tips. The male and female flowers are borne on separate plants. The seeds are brown, smooth-coated, slightly tapered with a feathery pappus. Canada thistle will grow anywhere, will adapt to mowed turf and will spread through its rhizomes.

Moss in lawns
Moss grows in lawns where the soil foodweb is changed from a bacterial-dominated system to a fungal-dominated system. Moss also grows in lawns with any of the following conditions:
• abundant shade and moisture
• poorly drained or compacted soil
• low soil fertility
• too low soil pH
• lack of air circulation.

You can choose to allow the moss to grow, or you can take steps to get rid of it.

To get rid of moss, you will need to correct the situation that allowed the moss to invade in the first place. Get your soil tested, including a foodweb assay. Rake up the existing moss and compost it or transplant it to other areas of your garden. Renovate your lawn and apply the appropriate soil amendments (based on soil tests). See page 141 for tips on dealing with shade.

Scouting for Disease
Scouting for disease is similar to scouting for weeds. Visually inspect small yards and use the transect method for large yards.

Disease thresholds
Disease thresholds are subjective. You will have to determine what level of damage is acceptable to you.

Disease control
Turfgrass diseases are always present in your lawn. They begin growth when the environmental conditions—including air temperature, relative humidity levels and time—are favorable for the disease to develop. All conditions must be met for disease to develop. Disease development can also be enhanced by problems in the soil, such as an imbalance of the soil foodweb, soil compaction or nutrient deficiencies.

You can do a number of things to reduce the incidence of disease in your lawn:
• Keep your soil foodweb healthy. A healthy foodweb keeps disease organisms in check.
• Do not overfertilize or overwater. Too much fertility results in lush growth that is susceptible to disease.
• Water in the morning so the grass blades can dry in the morning sun,

thus reducing the amount of time that moisture remains on the leaves.

- Do not cut the grass too short or leave it too long.
- Perform the necessary maintenance practices, such as aerating and thatch control, to keep the turfgrass as healthy as possible.
- Fix any low or high spots in the lawn and fix any drainage problems.
- Increase the amount of sunlight and airflow to the lawn.
- Plant turfgrasses that are disease resistant, that are adapted to your region or that are better adapted to shade.
- Remove the grass clippings from diseased areas to minimize the spread of disease.
- Do not walk through the diseased area and then onto other parts of your lawn.
- Clean any tools used on the diseased area before using them on another part of the lawn.
- Keep the lawn surface clear of debris, such as fallen leaves.
- Fallen leaves can also be shredded with a mulching mower and left on the lawn.

Turfgrass that is injured or under stress is susceptible to attacks by disease. Diseases often start as yellow, tan or brown patches of various sizes. However, these symptoms can also be caused by other things, and proper identification of the causal agent is important. Early identification makes the problem easier to deal with.

Liquid seaweed formulations are effective in preventing and fighting disease. Good-quality compost tea can also be effective in preventing disease outbreaks.

Removing leaves from the lawn in fall can reduce the incidence of disease.

Sample disease pest profile
Pink snow mold and fusarium patch
Microdochium nivale

Symptoms
Patches first appear as small, water-soaked spots less than 2" in diameter. Patches change color quickly from orange-brown to dark brown and finally to light gray. Patches usually grow to diameters of 8" or less, but can be larger. On closely mowed turf, a water-soaked, greenish-black margin may appear. Under snow or very wet conditions, white mycelium (masses of fungal strands) may be present on matted leaves. In sunlight, the mycelium and spore structures have a pinkish color. As snow melts, the patches appear bleached and may be confused with gray snow mold and other snow molds.

Favorable environmental conditions
Wet, humid conditions and temperatures between just above freezing and 60° F favor the development of this disease. Initial growth may be slow, but will advance rapidly under wet conditions. Pink snow mold needs snow cover and a long period of melting for severe outbreaks.

Disease/pathogen cycle
M. nivale survives unfavorable periods in infected grass plants or dead debris

as mycelia or conidia. When favorable conditions exist, mycelia grow from infected debris or from germinating conidia to infect leaves. Initial growth is slow, and infection may not be detected for several weeks. Infection spreads rapidly when conditions are right. The disease becomes inactive during warm, dry periods and can be easily transported as mycelia or spores by foot traffic and equipment.

ID

The name pink snow mold describes the disease when associated with snowmelt. Fusarium patch describes the disease when it occurs with no snow cover. A sample of the disease can be sent to a diagnostic lab, which will identify the disease for a reasonable fee. You can try to identify the disease by yourself with the use of a microscope, but that requires knowledge in the field of mycology. It's much easier to send your sample to a lab.

Susceptible turfgrasses

Annual bluegrass, Kentucky bluegrass and the bentgrasses are most susceptible. Kentucky bluegrass seldom suffers death from this disease.

When and how damage occurs

Damage can occur from fusarium patch after extended periods of high humidity in the leaf canopy. Pink snow mold develops under snow cover during the spring melt.

Scouting/monitoring

Scout for fusarium patch in the early morning when dew is present, and anytime during the day for pink snow mold. Look for active mycelium (fungal strands) on leaf tissue. Look for patches developing. Monitor the area on a weekly basis when unfavorable conditions exist and every two or three days when favorable conditions exist. Extra attention should be paid to areas that remain shaded for extended periods.

Threshold levels

Subjective.

Cultural controls

Allow your lawn to harden off for winter (allow the lawn to go dormant). Keep mowing your lawn into late fall. Remove or shred fallen leaves. Maintain adequate, balanced fertility—excess nitrogen will favor the disease. Avoid use of materials that raise the surface pH. Improve air movement through the area. Remove excess thatch. Overseed with disease-resistant cultivars. For fusarium patch, remove dew from the leaf blades in the early morning. This can be done with a long flexible pole or by dragging a garden hose across the lawn. For pink snow mold, control snow with fences. Spread out snowdrifts and encourage rapid melting of snow. Avoid snow compaction.

Biological controls

Spreading compost and spraying compost tea introduces a plethora of microorganisms to the turf surface. These microorganisms take up space, limiting the space available for disease to grow. They also use resources for their growth, limiting available resources for the disease. Spraying compost tea can effectively cover the leaf blades. Try it as a preventive spray for fusarium patch when conditions are favorable for disease development. Spreading compost on your lawn in fall could help reduce the incidence of pink snow mold.

Studies being done by Dr. Tom Hsiang of the Department of Environmental Biology at the University of Guelph in Ontario, Canada, have been focusing on the effects of a fungus *Typhula phacorrhiza* (related to gray snow mold), for the biological control of turfgrass snow molds, including gray snow mold and pink snow mold. The early results look promising. The efforts of scientists like Dr. Hsiang and others, with the focus moving away from chemical solutions, is a blessing for the health of our lawns and for the health of the planet.

If you feel the need to use chemical controls for any pest, consult a licenced pesticide professional.

Evaluation process

Evaluating your IPM program is an ongoing process. Fortunately for those of us in the northern and central US, we have the winter to do an in-depth evaluation. You can ask a number of questions to help in the evaluation. The more questions you ask, the better the evaluation.

- Was the monitoring program effective?
- Does the frequency of monitoring need to be increased, or can it be decreased?
- Were there any instances of the disease, in either form, seen during the year?
- If there were, was there enough damage to exceed your action threshold?
- Do you need to adjust your threshold level?
- Were your maintenance practices and control procedures effective, and do they need to be adjusted?
- Are there any new processes, products or information that could be of benefit in controlling this disease?
- Is there less damage this year than in previous years?

Notes on some other diseases to get you started on your pest profiles

Coprinus snow mold
Cottony Snow Mold, LTB, sLTB
Coprinus psychromorbidus
Prolonged periods of deep snow cover over frozen ground favor this disease. Optimal growth occurs at temperatures below 32° F, but growth may continue when temperatures rise above freezing. Damage is seen as rounded to irregular patches of woolly, white to gray mycelia in spring as the snow melts. The turfgrass blades become water-soaked or develop lesions that turn light brown with darker reddish brown margins when dry. Sclerotia (hardened survival/resting structures) serve as the survival mechanisms of the sclerotial strains. The survival mechanisms of the non-sclerotial strains are not known. Sclerotia start as conspicuous white hyphal knots, turning light brown and to dark brown upon maturity, and are found on the turfgrass blades or in the leaf sheaths. Most turfgrasses may be attacked. Some cultivars of Kentucky bluegrass are more susceptible than others.

Dollar spot

Lanzia and *Moellerodiscus* species
(*Sclerotinia homoeocarpa*)

Prolonged high humidity in the turf-grass canopy is required for dollar spot to develop. Favorable conditions for disease development include temperatures from 60–86° F, low nutrient availability, dry soils and humid days and cool nights that result in heavy dews. The fungus survives unfavorable periods as mycelia in infected plants and as stromata (hardened survival/resting structures) on leaf surfaces. The fungus can spread by movements of leaf debris, people, animals, water and wind. When the environmental conditions are favorable, the mycelia from within the infected tissue or from the stromata begin growing on the leaves. Mycelia may also grow out into the humid air, where they might contact a moist leaf surface, possibly infecting the leaf. Damage is seen as straw-colored patches from 1–6" across. The cobweb-like mycelia may be observed in the early morning when there is dew on the lawn. The leaves develop tan-colored spots or bands with darker, reddish brown borders in the early stages of the disease. All turfgrass species may be affected, with bent-grasses and bluegrasses being the most susceptible. Damage is usually not permanent.

Fairy ring

Basidiomycete soil fungi species

Fairy rings occur as a result of these fungi forming large colonies in the soil or thatch. Fairy ring fungi feed on dead organic matter, which releases nitrogen into the soil. This excess nitrogen often produces arched rings of lush grass that are darker green than the surrounding turfgrass. There may also be a dead area to the inside of the ring, and mushrooms may appear in the ring. The ring may also appear simply as an arch of mushrooms. Fairy rings are more active on lawns suffering from poor fertility and lack of water. The rings expand every year. Fairy ring can be dug out, but care must be taken to avoid spilling any soil on the unaffected lawn. Fairy ring fungi can be found as deep as 10' and the underground colony is often much wider than the ring you see on the lawn. The fungi can form a water-repellent mat in the soil that prevents water from infiltrating. When different fairy rings bump into each other, they inhibit each other's growth. Kentucky bluegrass and the bentgrasses are the most susceptible, but all turf-grass species may be affected.

Fairy ring can be difficult to manage, and the best strategy is to have a diverse, healthy and balanced soil food-web. Other things you can do include aerating to improve water infiltration, using a root feeder for trees to water the soil deeply and frequently, using a soaker hose to soak the rings and the surrounding area thoroughly for at least a month. Don't soak the area if living tree roots are present, as root rot may occur (and be careful of flooding into your basement).

Fairy ring mushrooms (and other mushrooms) will not damage your turfgrass but may affect the appearance. Some of these mushrooms are poisonous—pick and remove any mushrooms to minimize the danger to children and pets. However, removing the mushrooms will not control the spread of the ring. Removing any buried wood or old tree stumps will help alleviate the problem.

Helminthosporium leaf spot and melting out

Drechslera poae and *Bipolaris sorokiniana*

Leaf spot (*D. poae*) and melting out (*B. sorokiniana*) are similar diseases, and can cause similar symptoms in turfgrass. Conditions that favor these diseases include warm temperatures, excess thatch, excess nitrogen, lack of sunlight and mowing too close. Leaf spot, which is often seen in spring and fall, forms small to large irregular patches, and is observed as tan, red or purple spots on the leaves. The spots are longer than wide, but may stretch to the width of the blade, killing the leaf tip. Leaf sheaths are also attacked by leaf spot. Melting out is more often seen in summer, and is observed as spots on the leaf blades. The disease can move quickly down the blades and into the leaf sheaths, crowns and turfgrass roots, killing the plants. These diseases may affect all turfgrasses. Older Kentucky bluegrass cultivars are the most susceptible. New Kentucky bluegrass cultivars are often resistant.

Powdery mildew

Erysiphe graminis

Powdery mildew is mainly an aesthetic problem, but it can do serious harm if the infection is severe enough. It produces chains of conidia (specialized spores) in such profusion that the turfgrass leaves appear powdery. Powdery mildew overwinters as mycelium within living, infected plants. In areas with harsh winters, the fungus produces conidia and other spores that are embedded in infected plants or debris. The conidia are the primary source of the disease in turfgrasses. The conidia land on a susceptible plant and germinate quickly, with new conidia being produced in one week on newly infected plants. The conidia live only a few days but germinate over a wide range of temperatures from 34–86° F. The mycelia do not require a film of free moisture on the leaf surface. The disease is generally observed in spring and fall as conditions that favor powdery mildew include temperatures of 60–72° F, high humidity, shaded areas, areas with poor air circulation and extended periods of cloudy weather. Kentucky bluegrass is the most susceptible. Fine fescue may be affected.

Pythium blight

Pythium species

Pythium blight occurs during hot, humid weather. Conditions that favor pythium blight include daytime temperatures of 84–95° F, nighttime temperatures remaining above 68° F, moisture on the leaf blades for a minimum of 10 hours a day for a few consecutive days, excess thatch and high nitrogen levels. The disease appears as round to irregular patches 1–6" across, and can quickly grow. The leaves appear dark and water-soaked, and feel slimy in the early morning. The patches turn straw to brown in color, and matted leaves contain many disease spores. White, cottony mycelia may develop on the dead patches when moist. The crowns may be heavily damaged. Small, borderless, tan to orange spots develop on the leaf blades at the edge of the patches. The disease can be spread by mowing your lawn when it is wet and by surface runoff. Do not overwater or water when the leaf blades will remain moist for an extended time. The bentgrasses, annual bluegrass and perennial ryegrass are the most susceptible. Kentucky bluegrass may also be attacked.

Pythium root rot
Pythium species

All Pythium species that attack turf-grasses are self-fertile and produce spores as well as mycelia. Many species that cause root rot are active when temperatures are from 52–70° F, but the range extends from 32–90° F, depending on the species. Conditions required for disease development are the presence of water (standing water or locations where surface water runs off), compact soils that do not allow good water infiltration, low light levels and high nitrogen levels. The disease spores move rapidly through water and may spread the fungus through the surface drainage pattern. Damage may be noticed as yellowing, thinned patches or streaks in the lawn where there was standing water or surface water runoff. The roots will be short, brown, rotted and often infected with mycelia. The crowns may also be damaged. Mycelia are usually not present in the foliage. The disease can also move when infected plant tissue or infested soil is moved by humans, animals or machines. Annual bluegrass and the bentgrasses are the most susceptible. Tall fescue and perennial ryegrass may also be affected.

Red thread
Laetisaria fuciformis

The fungus forms a web-like, pale reddish mycelium that surrounds and connects the leaf blades. Red, orange or pink threads (a form of sclerotia) develop beyond the tips of the grass blades, and can be up to ⅜" long. Tiny spore-containing structures may form on dead, infected tissue. Red thread survives unfavorable growth periods in the form of sclerotia on infected leaves or in the thatch. Temperatures from 68–75° F, moisture-laden air and prolonged periods of leaf wetness favor disease development. The disease can develop at temperatures from 32–86° F. The disease can spread locally by water movement, machinery and foot traffic. A moisture film on the leaf surface is required for the disease to develop. The disease can kill leaves within two days of primary infection. Damage is seen as irregular patches of water-soaked leaves that turn straw-colored as the disease progresses. Fine fescues and perennial ryegrass are most susceptible, followed by Kentucky bluegrass. All turfgrass may be affected.

Rhizoctonia blight
Brown Patch
Rhizoctonia species

Rhizoctonia blight survives periods of unfavorable conditions as bulbils and monilioid cells (sclerotia-like survival structures) in plant debris. These structures are very tolerant of environmental extremes and pesticides. The different species and strains can germinate over a wide range of temperatures from 46–104° F. Conditions favorable for disease development include temperatures of 70–90° F, prolonged leaf wetness, high humidity, lush turfgrass growth and excess thatch. The disease spreads outward in the upper soil or thatch to form a roughly circular colony. Damage is observed as circular, straw-colored, often sunken patches, with the outer ring of the patch often appearing a smoky dark gray to dark purple in the early morning when dew is present. The patches can up to 3' across. Damage is not often permanent. The survival structures may be formed on or in infected turfgrass leaves and sheaths, and are liberated when the plant tissue decomposes. Prolonged periods of leaf wetness are necessary for severe damage to occur. Rhizoctonia species are capable of feeding on dead plant and animal matter in the soil. All turfgrasses can be affected. Tall fescue, annual bluegrass and the bentgrasses are most susceptible.

Snow scald
Myriosclerotinia borealis (Sclerotinia borealis)
This disease is favored by deep snow covering frozen ground. Damage is seen in spring as the snow melts. Look for patches of water-soaked leaves with gray mycelium and tan-colored sclerotia. Sclerotia may be spherical, oval or flake-like, and are found in the turfgrass blades or at the base of the plant. The mycelia bleach to white and the sclerotia mature to black. The disease is capable of growing at temperatures as low as 23° F, with 28° F being optimal for growth. Most turfgrasses are susceptible.

Summer patch
Magnaporthe poae
Summer patch overwinters as mycelia in previously colonized plant debris and in perennial host tissue. Disease infection begins when the soil temperature reaches 64–68° F. The fungus moves from plant to plant along roots and rhizomes. Visible symptoms develop during periods with 86–95° F temperatures and steady rain, or during periods of high temperatures following a heavy rainfall. The turfgrass will turn a dull green color, progressing to a straw color in small circular patches, 13/16–4" across that can grow to over 2' across. The patches are subject to invasion by weeds that thrive in hot weather, such as crabgrass, and by resistant turfgrass species, such as creeping bentgrass, giving the patch a 'frog-eye' appearance. The roots, crowns and rhizomes turn a dark brown color. Practices that reduce turfgrass stress and promote root development will aid in summer patch suppression. Annual bluegrass and Kentucky bluegrass are the most susceptible. Fine fescues may be affected.

Typhula blight
Gray Snow Mold
Typhula spp.
Typhula blight survives the summer as reddish brown to dark brown to black, round sclerotia, 3/32–3/8" in diameter. Use a hand lens to scout for sclerotia in early spring. Later on the sclerotia will dry and shrink and may be difficult to find. Pink snow mold does not produce sclerotia. Temperatures from 30–40° F, extended snow cover or moist conditions, and lush turfgrass growth in fall favor disease development. The disease stops growing when the temperature climbs above 45° F or when the turfgrass surface dries. Mycelial growth can occur under the snow. The disease appears as circular patches of often-matted turfgrass, straw to gray in color. Active gray-white mycelia can be seen on the edges of the patch. Sclerotia are produced on infected leaves or within leaf sheaths, and fall into the thatch as leaves decompose in spring. The disease tends to recur in the same area year after year if conditions are favorable. All turfgrasses can be affected. Perennial ryegrass, creeping bentgrass and annual bluegrass are most susceptible.

Snow mold problems commonly occur in years with prolonged snow cover. Snow molds get an early start when a wet, deep snow falls on unfrozen ground. Snow molds are often found growing along side each other.

Troubleshooting

IF YOUR LAWN IS DETERIORATING, YOU WILL HAVE TO FIND THE CAUSE, and then formulate an action plan to correct the cause. Depending on the source and extent of the problem, you can choose to repair, renovate or re-establish the lawn. Re-establishing a lawn requires more work than simple repair or renovation. See Lawn Installation on page 36 if the lawn has deteriorated to the point that re-establishment is required.

Pest Problems

Insects, disease or weeds may be causing your lawn to decline. If you have determined that pests have caused the deterioration, you will need to deal with that before proceeding with your repair, renovation or re-establishment. See the IPM section (pp. 102–137) for identifying and dealing with pests.

Non-pest Problems

There are a number of non-pest problems that can cause your lawn to deteriorate.

Summer dormancy

Cool-season grasses can go dormant in the summer, and your lawn may be entering dormancy (see p. 66). This is natural for cool-season turfgrasses that receive little to no irrigation, especially when the weather is hot. It is not a problem, just something to be aware of.

Lawn entering summer dormancy

Poor soil

The soil conditions may be too poor for good turfgrass growth. These conditions often appear as an overall loss of turfgrass vigor and change of color. Get your soil tested. There may be a problem with the soil chemistry, such as a nutrient deficiency and/or an imbalance in the soil foodweb that can be identified by a soil test or a foodweb assay. Soil amendments can be added during the renovation process. Good-quality compost tea can be sprayed on existing turf.

Nutrient deficiency

The chart below lists the nutrient deficiency symptoms of the three most used turfgrass nutrients plus iron chlorosis symptoms. Other nutrient deficiencies can be difficult to distinguish. A soil test is the only way to know for sure if your soil has a deficiency.

Compacted soil

The soil may be compacted. Most compaction on home lawns that are subject to foot traffic only occurs in the top 1–2" of the soil profile, which can easily be corrected with core aeration (see Aerating, p. 70). You can also check the soil profile. Dig down a couple of feet under the lawn to see what is happening in the rootzone. Use a spade to cut

Compacted lawn of low fertility

Healthy turfgrass resists compaction—its substantial root system takes a long time to develop a compacted layer under normal lawn usage.

the sod of a small area before you dig. To help keep the area clean, use a tarp or sheet of plywood to hold the diggings. If there is a layer of impervious hardpan deeper than 2", or a layer of soil that is texturally different that blocks air and water movement in the soil, you may need to re-establish your lawn. There are professional landscape contractors who have equipment that can penetrate 8" deep with minimal surface disruption. If foot traffic is creating a problem, take steps to redirect the traffic flow, or install a walkway. Low areas and depressions in the lawn, as well as areas where the soil remains moist, are more at risk for compaction.

NUTRIENT DEFICIENCY SYMPTOMS	
Nutrient	**Deficiency Symptoms**
nitrogen	pale green to golden yellow turf (yellowing begins in older blades)
phosphorous	lower, older blades turn very dark green, then dark blue-green to purple; plants are not vigorous
potassium	drooping of foliage; similar symptoms to water deficit; plants wilt immediately with lack of water; some yellowing between the leaf veins
iron	pale green to golden yellow turf (yellowing begins in younger blades); occurs in high pH soils, soils that have thick thatch and waterlogged soils

Temperature extremes

Hot and cold temperatures can cause lawns to decline. Be alert for weather that is really hot or unseasonably cold, and for drastic fluctuations in the weather. Not much can be done when it's too cold. However, for really hot days you can syringe your lawn during the hottest part of the day, which is simply applying a small amount of water to help lower the turfgrass temperature. Five minutes with a sprinkler is usually plenty for syringing.

Winter problems

Desiccation is the drying out of plant foliage and stems. Winter desiccation, which is caused by dry air or dry soil, occurs when the semi-dormant plants lose more moisture than they are able to absorb through the roots. Elevated areas, areas that lack snow cover, and air temperatures above 32°F exacerbate the drying out of the foliage. Winter desiccation can be prevented or lessened by making sure the soil moisture level is adequate before the ground freezes, by watering dry turf and by using a windbreak or mulch. Twiggy brush is good for mulch because the twigs help to trap snow and are easy to remove in spring.

Crown hydration occurs in late winter to early spring when turfgrass is stimulated by warm temperatures to begin growth, followed by quick drops in temperature to below freezing. The roots begin to take in water and the crowns become hydrated. The sudden temperature drop causes the water in the crowns to freeze, damaging the cells. Low spots, areas with poor drainage and areas with standing water are prone to crown hydration damage. Crown hydration can be mitigated by ensuring you have good surface drainage, by not overwatering in the late fall and by maintaining your lawn for good health.

Direct low-temperature kill occurs when the turfgrass is exposed to temperatures below its level of hardiness. Damage occurs most often when the turfgrass has not been allowed to harden off before winter and the turfgrass has no snow cover. Any practice that keeps the turfgrass lush and vigorous too late in the fall will increase the likelihood of direct low-temperature kill.

Chemical spills and problems

Fertilizer spills can upset the foodweb balance and can cause salt burn. This will often be seen as a dead, straw-colored patch surrounded by lush green turfgrass. For granular fertilizer spills, remove as much of the product from the area as you can. It can be reused. A wet/dry vacuum is a good tool for small spills. Spread the remaining product over as wide an area as

Dogs enjoy lawns in more ways than one!

possible with a broom or your hand. Flood the affected area with water to dilute the remaining product. For liquid fertilizer spills, flood the affected area with water a couple of times to dilute the spilled fertilizer. After the area has been flooded, proceed with lawn repair. You may have to dig out the offending bits.

Dog urine damage often looks like a fertilizer spill. The area will have a straw-colored dead area surrounded by lush green turf. Flood the area a couple of times with water to dilute and flush away any excess salts. Proceed with lawn repair. Take steps to keep dogs off your lawn.

Gas and oil are toxic to plants and soil life. If you are using gas-powered equipment, use caution when refilling, and never refill a lawnmower while it is on the lawn. Ensure your equipment is not leaking oil or gas. Refilling equipment should be done on a concrete surface, or other similar surface that is easy to clean up. Use a funnel to help avoid spills. If you do spill on the lawn, clean up the area immediately. An oil spill will look like a dark patch. A gas spill will create a straw-colored dead patch.

For gas and oil spills, the area may have to be dug up and the soil disposed of at a local eco-station or toxic waste facility. Small spots from oil or gas drops can be thoroughly soaked with water, then ignored; the turfgrass will eventually reclaim these spots. Dish soap can help break up an oil spill, but it can also spread the problem past the original damage site. New products on the market use microbial organisms to help clean up oil spills on lawns. Further research needs to be done into the effectiveness of these biological agents

and whether these microbial organisms will upset the balance of the existing soil foodweb.

If you have a pool, the chlorine can damage or kill the nearby turfgrass. The lawn will take on a yellow appearance. Flood the area with water to leach the chlorine deeper into the soil profile. You can then renovate the area, or if the damage is severe, consider re-establishment or installing a deck.

Buried debris

You might have buried debris in your lawn. Evidence of this can be seen as patches of dead or dormant grass while the remainder of the lawn remains green and healthy. Use a probe to check if there is something buried. You may have to dig that patch of lawn up to find the problem. Dead or dormant patches can also be a result of insect damage or overly thick thatch.

Poor maintenance

Improper maintenance practices can cause lawn deterioration. These can include mowing too short, too long or with a dull mower (dull mowers shred leaf tips); over or underwatering; or too much or too little fertilizer (see the Maintenance section, p. 58, for proper methods).

Lack of sunlight

The turfgrass might not be getting enough sun. For the best turfgrass performance, ensure your lawn gets at least six hours of sun per day. Turfgrass can grow in as little as four hours per day, but will not be as vibrant and healthy as lawns with more sun. It is possible that you or your neighbors have one or more trees that have grown up and are now shading the lawn. Perhaps a new

As trees & shrubs grow, the amount of shade over the lawn increases.

English ivy

building or addition has been constructed that now blocks the sun.

There are a number of things that can help when shade is a problem.

- Some species of turfgrass, such as fine fescues, perform better than other turfgrasses with reduced sunlight.
- Mow the turfgrass closer to the high end of the mowing range.
- Reduce the amount of water and fertilizer used for normal, full sun growing.
- Ensure that trees and shrubs have a mulched area around them at least out to the dripline of the tree or shrub.
- Prune out branches or remove whole trees.
- Build a path through the shaded areas to reduce traffic on the turfgrass.
- Deeply shaded areas are good candidates for other kinds of plants rather than turfgrass, such as those that thrive in shaded woodlands.

Ajuga

Groundcover plants for deep shade

Ajuga
Bugleweed
Ajuga reptans & *A. pyramidalis*
Ajuga features colorful foliage and late spring to early summer flowers in purple, blue, pink and white. Ajuga species grow 3–12" tall and 6–36" wide, and are hardy to Zone 3. Ajugas develop their best leaf color in partial or light shade but tolerate full shade. The leaves may be scorched with too much sun. Any well-drained soil is suitable. Divide plants any time during the growing season.

English ivy
Hedera helix
English ivy is a trailing groundcover or a climbing vine with dark, glossy, triangular evergreen leaves that may be tinged with bronze or purple in winter. As a groundcover it reaches about 12" in height and spreads indefinitely. It is hardy to Zone 5. English Ivy prefers light or partial shade but will adapt to any light conditions from full shade to full sun. The foliage can become damaged or dried out in winter if the plant is grown in a sunny, exposed site. The soil should be of average to rich fertility, moist and well drained.

Hosta
Plantain Lily
Hosta species, cultivars and hybrids
Hosta is a wonderful woodland perennial with decorative foliage and white to purple summer and fall flowers. Hostas grow 4–36" tall and 6"–6' wide, and are hardy to Zone 3. Hostas prefer light or partial shade but will grow in full shade. Morning sun is preferable to afternoon sun in partial shade situations. The soil should ideally be fertile, moist and well drained, but most soils are tolerated.

Japanese spurge

Hosta

Hostas are fairly drought tolerant, especially if given a mulch to help retain moisture. Division is not required but can be done every few years, in spring or summer, to propagate new plants. The dense growth and thick, shade-providing leaves of hostas make them useful for suppressing weeds.

Japanese spurge
Pachysandra terminalis
Japanese spurge is a durable, evergreen, perennial groundcover that grows about 8" tall and 12–18" wide or more. It bears inconspicuous white flowers in spring and is hardy to Zone 3. Pachysandras prefer light to full shade and tolerate partial shade. Any soil that is moist, acidic, humus rich and well drained is good. The foliage is considered evergreen but can look tired by spring. Remove old foliage to make way for new foliage.

Lily-of-the-valley
Convallaria majalis
Lily-of-the-valley is a perennial, mat-forming groundcover that grows 6–12" tall and spreads indefinitely. It produces fragrant, white or pink flowers in spring, and is hardy to Zone 2. Lily-of-the-valley grows well in full sun to full shade in humus rich, moist soil of average fertility, but most soils are tolerated. This plant is drought resistant. The pairs of leaves grow from small pips, or eyes, that form along the root. Divide a length of root into pieces, leaving at least one pip on each piece for propagation. Lily-of-the-valley can be quite invasive. Avoid planting them where you may later spend all your time trying to get rid of them.

Lily-of-the-valley

Periwinkle
Vinca minor

Periwinkle is a perennial groundcover that forms a low, loose mat of trailing stems with glossy, green foliage. It grows 4–8" tall and spreads indefinitely. Purple or blue flowers are borne mostly in spring, then sporadically all summer and into fall. It is hardy to Zone 4. Periwinkle grows well in partial to full shade in any type of soil as long as it is not too dry. Plants turn yellow if the soil is too dry or the sun too hot. Divide in early spring or mid- to late fall, whenever it becomes overgrown. One plant can cover almost any area. The use of mulch will help periwinkle thrive. It is shallow-rooted and able to outcompete weeds, but won't interfere with deeper-rooted shrubs.

Sweet woodruff

Sweet woodruff
Galium odoratum

Sweet woodruff is a perennial groundcover with fragrant, light green foliage. It grows 12–18" tall and spreads indefinitely. It bears star-shaped, white flowers in late spring to midsummer, and is hardy to Zone 3. Sweet woodruff prefers partial shade. It will grow well, but will not bloom well, in full shade. Soil should be humus rich and evenly moist. Shear back after blooming to encourage plants to fill in with foliage and crowd out weeds. The foliage smells like freshly mown hay, and the dried leaves were once used to scent bed linens and freshen stale rooms.

Variegated goutweed
Aegopodium podagraria 'Variegatum'

Variegated goutweed is a perennial groundcover that grows 8–24" tall and spreads indefinitely by rhizomes. It produces inconspicuous white flowers in summer and is hardy to Zone 3. It grows well in full sun to full shade in any well-drained soil. Soil of poor fertility is recommended to curb invasiveness. This plant is drought tolerant and thrives on neglect. Cut back or mow bedraggled foliage during the summer for fresh new growth to sprout. You will have to dig up any parts of the plant that are venturing into undesired

Periwinkle

Variegated goutweed

areas. Avoid planting goutweed near a lawn as it will quickly creep in.

Virginia creeper & Boston ivy
Parthenocissus quinquefolia & *P. tricuspidata*
Virginia creeper and Boston ivy are handsome, woody vines or groundcovers that establish quickly. They grow to about 12" tall as groundcovers, and can spread up to 70' wide. They grow well in any light from full sun to full shade in fertile, well-drained soil. The plants will adapt to clay or sandy soils. Virginia creeper has dark green foliage with each leaf divided into five leaflets, and is hardy to Zone 3. Boston ivy has dark green, three-lobed leaves, and is not quite as hardy as Virginia creeper. Fall color of both species is an attractive red.

Virginia creeper & Boston ivy

Lawn Repair
There are a couple of different methods for simple lawn repair.

For thin or bare patches, aerate the repair area with a core aerator or scratch the surface with a garden rake or garden weasel. Sprinkle some seed onto the area and scratch it again, ensuring the seeds are just covered with soil. If aerating, spread a light layer of screened compost over the seeded area and gently work the compost into the aeration holes. Treat the repaired area as new lawn.

If you are going to dig out an area, perhaps to remove perennial weeds or damage from a chemical spill, dig and remove the offending parts. Fill the area with soil that matches the existing soil. You can mix a small amount of compost into this soil. If seeding, the soil you are adding should be a little higher in elevation than the existing, undisturbed lawn (to allow for soil settling). You should be able to step onto the filled area from the undisturbed area and feel a slight elevation difference (hint: have your heel on the undisturbed soil and your toes on the filled soil). Sprinkle some seed over the area, scratch it in with a garden rake and treat the area as a newly seeded lawn. If sodding the repair area, fill the dug-out area with soil and a little compost. The filled soil level plus the new sod should be slightly higher in elevation than the undisturbed lawn to allow for soil settling. Treat as new sod.

If there are small, bare spots, such as those left after popping out dandelions, you can simply sprinkle a little turfgrass seed over the spot, add a light sprinkle of screened compost, then gently rub the area with the bottom of your foot or your hand. You can also

A simple lawn repair could fix the small, grassless area on this lawn.

Lawn Renovation

Lawn renovation entails improving your lawn beyond the normal level of maintenance, but not quite as radically as lawn re-establishment. The idea is to correct any problems and/or improve your lawn without having to tear up the whole thing. Do not expect instant results when renovating—it may take a couple or more years to see the results.

The renovation process is quite simple. After dealing with any pest or other problems identified by your IPM program, or if you are renovating to

Using a spade to cut an "H" over top of a depression in the lawn

Folding back cut pieces

Entire depression fully exposed

mix a small amount of seed and soil in a bucket or container for quick, spot seeding. Do not make extra, as the seed will germinate in the bucket after a few days. A watering wand or watering can is helpful to keep your repair areas moist without watering the whole lawn.

The following method is effective for leveling small bumps and hollows. Use a spade to cut an X or H into the soil, centering the cut over the center of the bump or hollow. The cuts should extend past the outer edges of the bump or hollow. Undercut the sod with the spade and peel the sod back. Shave down any bump with the spade or fill the hollow with soil similar to the existing soil. Fold the sod back over the area and step it down to ensure good sod-to-soil contact. Treat the repair as newly laid sod.

Shaving soil off sod pieces

Replacing cut pieces

simply improve your lawn, proceed as follows. Aerate in spring (April or May) or in fall (late August to mid-September) when the turfgrass is actively growing and has at least one month of active growth to recover after the renovation is complete. Use a core aerator, if possible. The soil should be moist but not wet or dry. Aerate the

lawn 2–5 times on the first day or within a couple of days from the start of the renovation, varying the direction of travel. Remove or break up the aeration plugs; breaking up the plugs removes the soil from the plug. Remove the remaining debris after breaking up the plugs. Overseed the lawn with a desirable turfgrass species, blend or mix that will thrive in your area and lawn situation. Topdress with good-quality compost at ½" thickness. Gently brush the compost into the aeration holes and down past the leaf blades. Roll the area with a water-filled roller to ensure good seed-to-soil contact. Water as for any newly seeded area (see Post-seeding Care, p. 50). Follow your normal mowing regime, as you will still have mature turf after the renovation is complete.

Adding soil to level depressed area

Levelling and smoothing added soil

Using feet to ensure good sod-to-soil contact

Turfgrass Maintenance Calendar

HERE IS A SIMPLE MAINTENANCE CALENDAR TO HELP YOU PLAN YOUR lawn maintenance regime. The dates will need to be adjusted to match your local climate and conditions.

January

Ensure lawn maintenance equipment is ready for spring. This is a good time to take power equipment in for servicing. Make sure all cutting blades are sharpened. Sharpen hand tools such as lawn edgers and shovels. Make sure you have enough line for your string trimmer.

Note: Do not use chemical de-icers on sidewalks or driveways next to lawn or garden areas.

February

Collect information on potential pests for your IPM pest profiles. Practice golf swing.

March

Watch the snow melt (if you have any). Large piles of snow can be spread around for even melting and watering of any exposed areas. Obtain or order supplies such as grass seed, fertilizer and compost. It is best to purchase compost close to the date of use. For example, you would not buy compost in spring for fall use. Begin IPM scouting. Scouting continues each month until the ground freezes.

April

Patience is a virtue. Wait until your lawn has dried out some before beginning the season's work. If the soil is too wet, you will be contributing greatly to soil compaction. De-thatch you lawn if necessary. Apply compost and fertilizer if you are performing those tasks in the spring. Water if necessary.

The best time to water turfgrass is first thing in the morning. Next best time is late in the evening. Avoid watering during the heat of the day, especially in the summer. Always water established lawns deeply. Deep watering creates deep rooting, which is less susceptible to environmental and physical stresses.

May

Begin mowing. Edge along sidewalks, driveways and flowerbeds. Aerate late in the month or in the beginning of June if necessary. Pull weeds as you see them. Water if necessary.

If you are using a string trimmer, always trim the lawn edges before you mow the lawn. Anything cut down by the string trimmer will be mulched or collected by the lawn mower.

June

Continue mowing and string trimming. Water when necessary. Pull weeds as you see them. Edge along sidewalks and driveways. Edge these areas once a month during the growing season for a manicured look. Some gardeners only edge once a year.

July

Continue mowing and string trimming. Water when necessary. Pull weeds as you see them. Edge along sidewalks and driveways.

Our grasses will enter summer dormancy in low water/high heat conditions. This is a survival mechanism of the grass. The grass looks brown but is not dead, and can be damaged if there is heavy traffic on it. Water deeply to bring the turfgrass out of dormancy; stay off it for a couple of days.

August

Continue mowing and string trimming. Water when necessary. Pull weeds as you see them. Edge along sidewalks and driveways.

September

Continue mowing and string trimming. Water when necessary. Pull weeds as you see them. Remove fallen leaves from lawn area and put them in the compost. Do fall aeration/thatch control around the middle of the month. Apply compost and organic granular fertilizer if needed. Collect and send soil samples for testing and a foodweb assay.

October

Mow and trim if necessary. Remove fallen leaves or shred leaves with a mulching mower and allow the shredded bits to remain on the lawn. Whole, matted leaves on the lawn reduce the amount of light that reaches the turfgrass and reduce air and water movement into the soil.

November

Drain oil and gas from power equipment. Remove any batteries and store them in the house. Make sure all your equipment is put away clean.

December

Evaluate the season's maintenance and IPM regimes. Begin planning for next year's lawn maintenance.

Low-maintenance Grasses and Legumes

Sheep fescue

For low-maintenance lawns, it is a good idea to choose grass species that are resistant to drought and disease, and that need little mowing, fertilizing or watering. The soil preparation for a low-maintenance lawn is essentially the same as for a higher-quality lawn, keeping in mind the conditions the low-maintenance grass species need to thrive. The following is a selection of some grasses and legumes used in low-maintenance applications.

Low-maintenance grasses
Hard fescue
Festuca duriuscula (*F. longifolia*, *F. ovina* var. *duriuscula*)
Hard fescue is a dense, fine-textured, cool-season, bunch-type grass that spreads by tillers. The leaves range from gray-green to dark green to blue-green, and tend to flop over, which gives the appearance of shorter turf. The abundant leaves and roots make hard fescue an excellent species for erosion control and soil remediation. Hard fescue

grows well in full sun in well-drained soils of low fertility. Hard fescue tolerates drought, heat and shade, and is resistant to many diseases. It tends to hold its color better over the summer than other fine fescues. Wear tolerance is good but recuperative potential is poor. Hard fescue can be used on its own or as part of a low-maintenance lawn mixture. New cultivars can be included in a medium-maintenance lawn, and can be mowed at a height of 2–6".

Sheep fescue
Festuca ovina
Sheep fescue is another dense, fine-textured, cool-season, bunch-type grass that spreads by tillers. The leaves are bright green to blue-green in color, and very stiff. Sheep fescue does well in full sun in well-drained, acidic, sandy or gravelly soils of poor fertility. It is very tolerant of cold and drought, tolerant of shade, resistant to many diseases and somewhat tolerant of heat. Wear tolerance is good but recuperative potential is poor. Sheep fescue is also used for erosion control and soil remediation. It is often included as part of a low-maintenance mixture and can be used on its own. It can be mowed in the 2–3" range.

Canada bluegrass
Poa compressa
Canada bluegrass is a medium-textured, erect, cool-season grass that spreads by rhizomes. The leaves are bluish green. Canada bluegrass grows best in full sun in poorly drained soils of low fertility, but can adapt to most soils. It has excellent cold tolerance and is tolerant of shade and drought. The compact, creeping growth habit makes Canada bluegrass a good choice for erosion control, and for areas where very minimal maintenance is necessary. It can be used alone or as part of a low-maintenance mixture. The seeds need direct light for germination. Canada bluegrass can be mowed in the 2–6" range.

Rough bluegrass
Poa trivialis

Rough bluegrass is a soft, dense, fine-textured, cold-hardy, cool-season, bunch-type grass that spreads by stolons. The green foliage often retains its color over the winter in milder climates. Rough bluegrass grows well in full sun to partial shade to light shade in moist soils of less than perfect drainage. Rough bluegrass is tolerant of wet soils. It can outcompete the more desirable Kentucky bluegrass and perennial ryegrass in full sun, and has a lower fertility requirement than Kentucky bluegrass. It has medium to poor wear tolerance, but can recover quickly from injury. Rough bluegrass can produce a good-quality, uniform stand on its own, and can be used in medium-maintenance situations. It can also be used in low-maintenance and shade mixtures. Light, frequent irrigation and mowing at 2" or less will favor rough bluegrass. It can be mowed as short as ¼".

Blue grama grass
Bouteloua gracilis

Blue grama grass is a low-growing, cold-hardy, fine-textured, warm-season, bunch-type turfgrass that spreads by tillers. It has light green to gray-green leaves. Blue grama grass grows well in full sun in well-drained, neutral to alkaline soil, but can adapt to a wide range of soils. Blue grama grass has good drought tolerance, fair salinity tolerance and good tolerance of wide temperature fluctuations, such as those produced by chinooks off the eastern slopes of the Rocky Mountains. Blue grama grass is not tolerant of shady locations and wet or acidic soils. It is a very important native short and tall grass prairie species, making up the majority of the grass population there. It is slow to become established. It has moderate wear tolerance, but is slow to recover from injury. The dense roots work well for erosion protection. It will go dormant in summer under drought conditions. It can be used on its own or in a 2:1

mixture with buffalograss. With mowing, the tufts grow together and form a thick sod. Mow at a height of 2–3".

Buffalograss
Buchloe dactyloides

Buffalograss is a short, soft, fine-textured, warm-season turfgrass that spreads by stolons, and has separate male and female plants. The light green to bluish gray leaves of buffalograss tend to green up later than other grasses, and tend to go dormant with the first hard frost. Buffalograss grows best in full sun in moderate to fertile, well-drained soils. Buffalograss adapts well to clay soils and soils with poor drainage. It is quite tolerant of heat, and is tolerant of short-duration floods, but does not tolerate too much shade or soils with excessive drainage. Buffalograss has great drought resistance owing to its deep, extensive, root system, and may only need water once in the summer to prevent dormancy. It has good wear tolerance and good recovery potential. Buffalograss is not hardy in all parts of the northern and central US, but it has better cold hardiness than other warm-season

Buffalograss

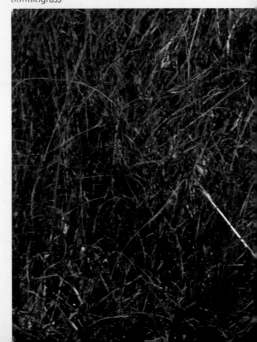

turfgrasses, with some cultivars more cold tolerant than others. Buffalograss seed is more expensive than most other turfgrass species. It mixes well with blue grama grass, and can be used on its own. Mow at 2–4" for home lawns, and taller or not at all for very low-maintenance areas.

Redtop
Agrostis alba (*A. gigantea*)
Redtop is a medium- to coarse-textured, cool-season turfgrass that spreads by short rhizomes. Redtop is related to the bent-grasses. It has medium green to blue-green foliage, and its reddish flowers give rise to the common name. Redtop grows best in full sun in moist, acidic soils, but can tolerate a wide range of soils, including wet and poorly drained soils. Redtop adapts well to humid conditions, but may not perform as well in drought, heat and shade. It lacks the cold hardiness of the other *Agrostis* species, and often regenerates by seed where it is not hardy. It has poor wear tolerance and recovery potential. It forms sod quickly, and is used as a nurse grass or as part of a low-maintenance mixture. Redtop can be mowed at 2–3".

Fairway wheatgrass
Crested wheatgrass
Agropyron cristatum
Fairway wheatgrass is a cold-hardy, drought-tolerant, fine- to medium-textured, cool-season, bunch-type turfgrass that spreads by short rhizomes. It greens up early in spring, but tends to go dormant in heat and drought. Fairway wheatgrass grows well in full sun in a wide range of soils as long as there is some drainage. Fairway wheatgrass establishes quickly, and the dense, extensive, fibrous root system, which can grow 4–8' deep, makes this plant good for erosion protection and soil remediation. Fairway wheatgrass can withstand moderate flooding in spring, but will suffer in poorly drained soils or with too much irrigation. It mixes well with other low-maintenance grasses, but

will outcompete native grasses. It can be mowed at a height of 3–4".

Low-maintenance legumes
Crown vetch
Coronilla varia
Crown vetch is a rhizomatous, herbaceous perennial legume with dark green leaves and prostrate stems that grow to 1–2' tall and 2–6' wide. It produces attractive, white to pink flowers in summer. Crown vetch grows best in full sun in well-drained, neutral to slightly acidic soil of poor fertility. It has good drought tolerance and fair shade tolerance, and adds nitrogen to the soil. It does well in rocky, gravelly areas, and can adapt to a range of soils. It can be difficult to mow and can be invasive in fertile, moist soil. It is best used in areas that require no mowing, such as on steep slopes, other areas where erosion protection is important and very low-maintenance, out of the way areas. It can be used alone and seeded at $^1/_2$–1 lb/1000 ft^2. It can also be mixed with bird's foot trefoil and most of the low-maintenance grasses listed above, except blue grama grass and buffalograss. It can be slow to establish by seed, but can also be propagated using pieces of the rhizomes.

Bird's foot trefoil
Lotus corniculatus
Bird's foot trefoil is a semi-erect, herbaceous perennial legume with green foliage and attractive yellow flowers that are borne in spring to early summer. It grows 12–16" tall. Bird's foot trefoil grows best in full sun in well-drained, slightly alkaline to slightly acidic soil of poor fertility. It has excellent drought tolerance and fair shade tolerance, and also adds nitrogen to the soil. It does well in rocky, gravelly areas, and can adapt to a range of soils, including poorly drained soils. Bird's foot trefoil also tolerates heat and salty conditions. It is used in the same situations as crown vetch, but it tolerates occasional mowing. It is faster to establish than crown vetch, and can be seeded alone at $^1/_4$–$^1/_2$ lb/1000 ft^2.

Common Turfgrass Weeds

Common name	Botanical name	Life length	Plant type	Growth habit	Spreads by
barnyardgrass	Echinochloa crusgalli	annual	grass	bunch	seeds, creeping stems
bedstraw	Galium spp.	annual	broadleaf	creeping	seeds
broadleaf plantain	Plantago major	perennial	broadleaf	bunch	seeds
buffalobur	Solanum rostratum	annual	broadleaf	bunch	seeds
Canada thistle	Cirsium arvense	perennial	broadleaf	creeping	rhizomes, seeds
carpetweed	Mollugo verticillata	annual	broadleaf	creeping	seeds
chickweed	Stellaria media	annual	broadleaf	creeping	seeds, creeping stems
crabgrass	Digitaria spp.	annual	grass	bunch	seeds
creeping bellflower	Campanula rapunculoides	perennial	broadleaf	creeping	rhizomes, seeds
creeping buttercup	Ranunculus repens	perennial	broadleaf	creeping	seeds, runners
field horsetail	Equisetum arvense	perennial	broadleaf	creeping	rhizomes, spores
field sandbur	Cenchrus pauciflorus	annual	grass	bunch	seeds
goutweed	Aegopodium podagraria	perennial	broadleaf	creeping	rhizomes, seeds
green foxtail	Setaria viridis	annual	grass	bunch	seeds
ground ivy	Glechoma hederacea	perennial	broadleaf	creeping	seeds
Johnson grass	Sorghum halepense	perennial	grass	creeping	seeds, rhizomes
lamb's-quarters	Chenopodium album	annual	broadleaf	bunch	seeds
mayweed	Anthemis cotula	annual	broadleaf	bunch	seeds
orchardgrass	Dactylis glomerata	perennial	grass	bunch	seeds
pineapple weed	Matricaria matricarioides	annual	broadleaf	bunch	seeds
prostrate knotweed	Polygonum aviculare	annual	broadleaf	creeping	seeds
puncturevine	Tribulus terrestris	annual	broadleaf	creeping	seeds
quackgrass	Agropyron repens	perennial	grass	creeping	rhizomes, seeds
sheep sorrel	Rumex acetosella	perennial	broadleaf	creeping	seeds, rhizomes
shepherd's purse	Capsella bursa-pastoris	annual	broadleaf	bunch	seeds
stinkweed	Thlaspi arvense	annual	broadleaf	bunch	seeds
violets	Viola spp.	perennial	broadleaf	creeping	seeds
witchgrass	Panicum capillare	annual	grass	bunch	seeds
yellow woodsorrel	Oxalis stricta	perennial	broadleaf	creeping	seeds

Glossary

acuminate: tapering to a sharp point

aerobic: with or in the presence of oxygen

aggregate: a stable collection of particles

aggregation process: the process of particles coming together to form an aggregate

anaerobic: without or not in the presence of oxygen

auricle: turfgrass leaf appendages that grow out from the collar

blade: the upper portion of a turfgrass leaf

blend: a stand of turfgrass with two or more cultivars of the same species

bract: a modified leaf that appears just under the flower or flowers

budshoot: the leaf bud, composed of new leaves in either a rolled or folded arrangement in cross-section

bunch-type grass: turfgrass that has an upright, clumping habit

chlorosis: leaf yellowing owing to loss of chlorophyll

commercial inoculum: commercially available bacteria and fungi used for re-establishing healthy populations of soil organisms

compost: decomposed organic matter

crown: the main growing point of a turfgrass plant

diazinon: an organophosphate insecticide currently being phased out of usage because of unacceptable health hazards to children

dormant: at rest; suspended biological activity

dripline: the area around the bottom of the tree, directly under the tips of the farthest extending branches

early successional plants: often the first plants to invade and grow in a disturbed area

fish hydrolysate: a liquid product for plant nutrition made from sliced, diced and ground enzymatically digested fish

foodweb assay: an evaluation of the presence and numbers of soil microorganisms and soil macroorganisms, such as bacteria, fungi and nematodes

hardpan (impervious hardpan): a layer of compacted soil that develops at certain depths under the soil, which disrupts air and water movement and restricts root growth.

keeled: having a keel, such as is seen on the bottom of a canoe

lignin: a plant chemical, related to cellulose, that helps form woody cell walls and provide plant rigidity

ligule: thin appendage extending up from the leaf sheath where the leaf blade meets the leaf sheath

mixture: a stand of turfgrass composed of two or more species and cultivars

monostand: a stand of grass of only one cultivar

mycology: the study of fungi and fungal pathogens

mycorrhizal fungi: root-colonizing fungi that form symbiotic relationships with the plants to which they have attached themselves

nurse crop: for lawns, a turfgrass species that germinates and establishes quickly from seed, providing shelter and erosion protection for the newly seeded area until the desirable turfgrass species become established

organic: of, relating to, or derived from living organisms

organophosphate: a class of insecticides that contain organic phosphorus compounds whose mode of action is to inhibit the neurotransmitter acetylcholinesterase

overseeding: spreading turfgrass seed over an already established lawn

polystand: a stand of turfgrass composed of more than one species or cultivar

protozoa: single-celled organisms that feed on soil bacteria and help release nutrients held in the bodies of the bacteria

raster: the anterior (front side) of the last abdominal segment of a white grub

rhizomatous grass: turfgrass that spreads vegetatively by rhizomes

rhizomes: underground lateral shoots that arise from the turfgrass crown

rootzone: the top layer of a soil profile where the majority of plant roots grow

scalped: turfgrass plants that have been cut too short

sheath: the lower part of a turfgrass leaf

shoot: stem and leaves of a turfgrass plant

soil foodweb: hierarchical food chain consisting of living and dead soil flora and fauna, plants and aboveground animals

soil parent material: the substrate that the mineral portion of the soil is derived from

stand: an area of turfgrass

stoloniferous grass: turfgrass that spreads vegetatively by stolons

stolons: aboveground lateral shoots that arise from the turfgrass crown

subgrade: the layer of earth (clay, rock) that the topsoil rests upon

tillering grass: turfgrass that spreads vegetatively by tillers

tillers: upright lateral shoots that branch off of the primary shoot, just above the crown, to form new plants

topdressing: the application of a thin, even layer of compost or soil over the lawn surface

volatilization: the vaporization of a substance, which then diffuses into the air

Resources

Books and publications

Alex, J.F. 1992. *Ontario Weeds*. Ontario Ministry of Agriculture and Food Publication 505, Guelph, ON.

Beard, James B. 1973. *Turfgrass: Science and Culture*. Prentice-Hall, Inc., Englewood Cliffs, NJ.

Danneberger, T.K. 1993. *Turfgrass Ecology and Management*. Lawn and Landscape Maintenance, Cleveland, OH.

Eggens, J.L. 1992. *Turf Management: Principles and Practices Study Guide*. Department of Horticultural Science, University of Guelph, Guelph, ON.

Ellis, B.W. and F.M. Bradley, eds. 1996. *The Organic Gardener's Handbook of Natural Insect and Disease Control*. Rodale Press, Emmaus, PA.

McDonald, David K. 1999. *Ecologically Sound Lawn Care for the Pacific Northwest: Findings from the Scientific Literature and Recommendations from Turf Professionals*. City of Seattle Public Utilities, Seattle, WA. Also online at http://www.seattle.gov/util/stellent/groups/public/@spu/@rmb/@csd/@rescons/-documents/spu_informative/ecological_200312021255394.pdf.

McKernan, Dennis. 1994. *Great Plains Turfgrass Manual*. Life Works Design and Consulting, Olds, AB.

Rubin, Carole. 1990. *How to Get Your Lawn & Garden Off Drugs: Pesticide-free Gardening for a Healthier Environment*. Harbour Publishing, Madeira Park, BC.

Schumann, Gail L. et. al. 1997. *IPM Handbook for Golf Courses*. Ann Arbor Press, Chelsea, MI.

Scott's Guide to the Identification of Turfgrass Diseases and Insects. 1987. O.M. Scott & Sons Company, Marysville, OH.

Sears, M., T. Hsiang and P. Charbonneau. 1996. *Diseases and Insects of Turfgrasses in Ontario*. Ontario Ministry of Agriculture and Food Publication Publication 162, Guelph, ON.

Smiley, R.W. P.H. Dernoeden and B.B. Clarke. 1992. *Compendium of Turfgrass Diseases, 2nd Edition*. American Phytopathological Society, St. Paul, MN.

Turfgrass websites

These are very good websites for United States turfgrass information. There are also good websites from a number of Canadian sources. Use a search engine such as google.com or dogpile.com and search criteria such as turfgrass, natural lawns, organic lawns, turfgrass IPM, lawn IPM, turfgrass pests, turfgrass seed to find this information. For individual pests or plant species, make the search criteria specific to the pest or plant.

Composting Council of Canada
www.compost.org

Guelph Turfgrass Institute
http://www.uoguelph.ca/GTI/index.html

Jacklin Seed
www.simplot.com/turf/jacklin

National Turfgrass Evaluation Program
Seed testing and evaluation over a wide range of climates and geographical locations. www.ntep.org/contents2.shtml

New Brunswick Horticulture Trades Association
http://www.nbhta.ca/Turf_Manual.htm

Pennsylvania State University Turfgrass Management and Extension
http://turfgrassmanagement.psu.edu/

The Lawn Institute, Rolling Meadows, IL, has loads of information.
http://www.LawnInstitute.com and http://www.TurfGrassSod.org

United States Composting Council
http://www.compostingcouncil.org/index.cfm

Foodweb assay

Soil Foodweb, Inc.
728 SW Wake Robin Avenue, Corvallis, OR 97333
phone: (541) 752-5066 fax: (541) 752-5142
info@soilfoodweb.com

Paul J. Wagner
Soil Foodweb New York, Inc.
555 Hallock Ave. (rte 25a), Suite 7
Port Jefferson Station
New York 11776
phone: 631-474-8848
fax: 631 474-8847
soilfoodwebny@aol.com

Endnotes
for "Some Good Reasons Not To Use Pesticides" (pp. 103–108)

1. Aspelin, A.L. 1997. Pesticides industry sales and usage: 1994 and 1995 market estimates. U.S. EPA. Office of Prevention, Pesticides and Toxic Substances. Office of Pesticide Programs. Biological and Economic Analysis Division. Washington, D.C., Aug.

2. Landrigan, P.J. *et al.* 1999. "Pesticides and inner-city children: Exposures, risks, and prevention." Environmental Health Perspectives 107 (Suppl. 3):431-437.

3. Aspelin, A.L. and A. H. Grube. November 1999. Pesticides industry sales and usage: 1996 and 1997 market estimates. U.S. Environmental Protection Agency (EPA). Office of Prevention, Pesticides, and Toxic Substances. Office of Pesticide Programs. Biological and Economic Analysis Div, pp. 21-22. www.epa.gov/pesticides. The 28 pesticides whose estimated use is over 5 million lbs per year are atrazine, metolachlor, 2,4-D, metam sodium, glyphosate, methyl bromide, dichloropropene, acetochlor, paradichlorobenzene, pendimethalin, trifluralin, chlorpyrifos, cyanazine, alachlor, copper hydroxide, chlorothalonil, dicamba, mancozeb, EPTC, terbufos, dimethenamid, bentazon, propanil, simazine, copper sulfate, DEET, MCPA and chloropicrin.

4. U.S. EPA. 1987–2000. "Integrated risk information system." www.epa.gov/iris. (Files for acetochlor, alachlor, atrazine, bentazon, bromomethane [methyl bromide], chlorothalonil, chlorpyrifos, 2,4-dichlorophenoxyacetic acid (2,4-D), dicamba, 1,4-dichlorobenzene, 1,3-dichloropropene, s-ethyl dipropylthiocarbamate (EPTC), glyphosate, 2-methyl-4-chlorophenoxyacetic acid (MCPA), metolachlor, pendimethalin, propanil, simazine, and trifluralin. Only for 1,3-dichloropropene did no tests show evidence of reproductive problems.)

5. Canadian Centre for Occupational Health and Safety bulletin. 1990. Ottawa, ON.

6. Environment Canada. 1989. "Pesticides, the right amount." Ottawa, ON.

7. U.S. EPA. January 23, 1995. "Analysis of chlorpyrifos IDS data for domestic animals." Memo from V. Dobozy to B. Kitchens, Occupational and Residential Exposure Branch. www.epa.gov/pesticides.

8. Hayes, H.M. et al. 1991. "Case-control study of canine malignant lymphoma: positive association with dog owner's use of 2,4-dichlorophenoxyacetic acid herbicides." *Journal of the National Cancer Institute*, 83:1226-1231.

9. U.S. Geological Survey. 1999. "The quality of our nation's waters: nutrients and pesticides." Circ. 1225, p. 58.

10. Majewski, M.S. and P.D. Capel. 1995. *Pesticides in the atmosphere: distribution, trends, and governing factors.* Ann Arbor Press, Inc., Chelsea MI: pp. 78-79.

11. The 10 pesticides whose use is estimated by the U.S. EPA to harm fish or birds are atrazine, metolachlor, dichloropropene, pendimethalin, trifluralin, chlorpyrifos, alachlor, chlorothalonil, terbufos and bentazon. The risk assessments for fish and birds are found in the following documents: U.S. EPA. 2001. "Reregistration eligibility science chapter for atrazine: Environmental fate and effects chapter," pp. 7,8; U.S. EPA. 1995. "Prevention, Pesticides and Toxic Substances. Reregistration eligibility decision: metolachlor," p. 33; U.S. EPA. 1998. "Prevention, Pesticides and Toxic Substances. Reregistration eligibility decision: 1,3-dichloropropene," p. 77; U.S. EPA. 1997. "Prevention, Pesticides and Toxic Substances. Reregistration eligibility decision: pendimethalin," p. 88; U.S. EPA. 1996. "Prevention, Pesticides and Toxic Substances. Reregistration eligibility decision: Trifluralin," pp. 56,59; U.S. EPA. 2000. "Reregistration eligibility science chapter for chlorpyrifos: Fate and environmental risk assessment chapter," p. 101; U.S. EPA. 1998. "Prevention, Pesticides and Toxic Substances. Reregistration eligibility decision: alachlor," p. 173; U.S. EPA. 1999. "Prevention, Pesticides and Toxic Substances. Reregistration eligibility decision: chlorothalonil," pp. 131, 142; U.S. EPA. 1999. "Revised Environmental Fate and Effects Division reregistration eligibility decision chapter for terbufos," pp. 36, 39; and U.S. EPA. 1993. Office of Prevention, Pesticides and Toxic Substances. "Reregistration eligibility decision: bentazon" p. 30. All can be found on the EPA website at www.epa.gov/pesticides/reregistration/status.htm.

12. See endnote 1.

13. Potter, D.A. et al. 1990. "Toxicity of pesticides to earthworms (Oligochaeta: Lumbricidae) and effect on thatch degradation in Kentucky bluegrass turf." *Journal of Economic Entomology* 83:2362-2369.

14. FIFRA Sec. 3(c)(5)(C)

15. 40 CFR § 156.10 (g) (U.S. Code of Federal Regulations Title 40—Protection of Environment).

16. 40 CFR § 158.340.

Index of main topics

About the Author

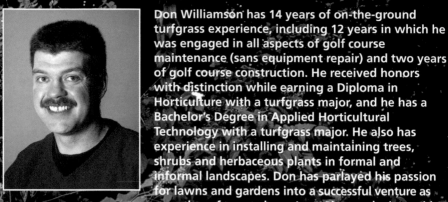

Don Williamson has 14 years of on-the-ground turfgrass experience, including 12 years in which he was engaged in all aspects of golf course maintenance (sans equipment repair) and two years of golf course construction. He received honors with distinction while earning a Diploma in Horticulture with a turfgrass major, and he has a Bachelor's Degree in Applied Horticultural Technology with a turfgrass major. He also has experience in installing and maintaining trees, shrubs and herbaceous plants in formal and informal landscapes. Don has parlayed his passion for lawns and gardens into a successful venture as co-author of over a dozen Lone Pine gardening guides.